My Journey to Paradise

By

Dr. Heng Lim
with
V.S. Mitchell

This book is dedicated to my wife Ra,
who is the love of my life
and the wind beneath my wings.

Foreword

We all know the old saying, "Where there's life, there's hope." Without hope, life is impossible. How can we survive without at least a spark of possibility? How can we grow unless hope keeps us looking, learning and moving forward? That's what hope is, after all—the desire and ability to move forward. It's a forward-looking attitude and a forward-moving orientation. Oh, how we need hope!

Not many of us have the privilege of knowing someone who has the kind of hope that carries them through difficult and dangerous times. Dr. Heng Lim is one of those special people. His life speaks of hope. He is a rich and rare blend of personal intensity, scriptural integrity, contagious joy—and hope. His life story is one of hope.

Dr. Lim is well qualified to speak to us on this subject. Think of all the improbable places in history where hope survived—The Holocaust in Germany, the American Civil War, the Killing Fields of Cambodia. Human hope is hard to kill, but it can be killed. It can run out of strength. It can drain out into despair and depression. That is why we need a hope stronger than death—the hope that God gives. Dr. Heng Lim's life shows us, "Where there's hope, there's life." As his pastor and friend, I can tell you that he does indeed have hope—hope that finds its Source in God. I am happy to recommend this book to you. May it spark hope in your soul.

Rev. Linzy Sladen, pastor,
Friendship Baptist Church,
Owasso, Oklahoma

A Word from the Editor

When I heard Dr. Lim share some excerpts from his life story, I knew that it was story worth knowing, and I asked him to consider writing it. It turned out that my request was merely an echo of hundreds of requests that had preceded it, and he was already well along with a manuscript. When he finished it, Linda Fisher, a fellow member of Friendship Baptist Church, graciously typed it into a word processor file. Believing that the world needed to hear Dr. Lim's story, I asked if he would allow me to edit it in preparation for publication. Having worked through every line of it, I am even more convinced that it will open the eyes of many to what the grace of God can do, even in the most desperate of circumstances. I consider it a privilege to know Dr. Lim and to assist in bringing his story into print.

V.S. Mitchell

Preface

For years I have wanted to write a story about how God, with His grace and mercy, saved my family and me from the "killing fields" of Cambodia and brought me to America, the wonderful country I now call home. God bless America! I have attempted to write this story many times. At one time I even completed it, but the editor lost the three-hundred page manuscript. Several hundred people—if not thousands—have encouraged me to write my story. They said it would bring encouragement and blessing to those who would read it.

Since I graduated from dental school in 1994, God has allowed me to speak in many churches and conferences. He has also allowed me to distribute over 35,000 copies of my profile, which was written by the dean of the dental school, Dr. Frank Miranda. The story was featured in the first issue of Oklahoma University Alumni Magazine under the title, "From the Killing Fields to the Healing Art".

I believe that the Lord has a right time for everything, and that's why He did not allow me to publish this story until now. These are my goals in writing this story:

1. To point people to God;
2. To help people see more clearly the opportunity for salvation that we have in Christ;

3. To encourage people to make the most of the abundant opportunities we have as citizens of the free world;
4. To help people recognize that God's blessing is everywhere, even in times of trouble;
5. To motivate people to learn from their past;
6. To show that, regardless of our circumstances, with God's help we can become better people.

With these goals in mind I would like to share with you my story of how God, in His mercy, saved me from death in Cambodia and brought my family and me to America. As I look back on my life, with all its troubles and dangers, I have to believe that it was God and His providence that saved me! After you read my story, you will believe it, too.

—Dr. Heng Lim

Contents

CHAPTER 1

The Early Days

I was born in a small town named Kendal, in the province of Tekvil, 20 miles south of Phnom Penh, the capital of Cambodia. Because the town was small, everyone knew everyone else. A two-lane asphalt highway ran through the middle of town. My house was sandwiched between a river and the highway. It was a small, humble home with a tin roof. During the monsoon season the raindrops beat against the roof, creating a soothing melody that was music to my ears. I loved listening to the sound of the falling rain. In front of the house was a market, the main place in town for the buying and selling of meats and vegetables. My father and mother owned a little butcher shop there.

Less than half a block south from the house was a Buddhist temple. Surrounding the Buddhist temple was a concrete wall covered with exotic yellow, pink and red flowers. My big brother Cheang and I used to climb over this wall to visit the high priest, whom we greatly loved and respected. His name was Nate. To reach the building where the high priest lived, we had to run through a courtyard filled with above-ground tombs. I did not dare to go there alone, because I had heard so many ghost stories from other local boys. The high priest knew about our fear, and he often reminded us that he had said special prayers to keep the ghosts from bothering us. He showed us a white thread, which looked like ordinary sewing thread, and said, "This thread looks small and weak, but with special prayer it can bind the mighty ghost, and he can not escape me." I believed him. He also said that there was a demon named Amouk, who could stand as tall as the tallest palm tree. His legs were so long that he could step over the Buddhist Temple. He lived in a place called hell. High priest Nate told us that there is also a place called heaven, where angels and God live. He taught us that if we would try to do good deeds, our lives would be blessed, but if we practiced evil things, our lives would be cursed. Along with my parents, the priest taught us morals and discipline. There were many young boys there, but we were his favorites. The high priest gave us nicknames. Cheang's nickname was "Akang", and mine was "Akom". To this day I do not know what they mean.

My maternal grandfather and his family also lived in the Tekvil province; their home was about two miles south from ours. I used to walk along the riverbank to visit Grandpa's place. Those were the best of times! One could know without a doubt where our grandfather's house was, because his was the only house in the area that didn't have anything growing in the front yard. This was a very unusual sight, because Cambodia is a tropical country, and plants and trees grow everywhere. The dirt around his house was as white as sand on a beach.

My grandfather owned a grocery store there, and also a turnip-processing place. Every summer, ox-cart loads of fresh, white turnips would be brought to his house. Grandpa hired local villagers to cut the turnips into pieces with knives. They would throw the pieces into a bowl-shaped hole in the ground that was almost as big as a swimming pool. Then they would pour salt on top of the turnips to marinate and preserve them. The workers would take off their shoes, climb into the hole and walk all over the salt and turnips, massaging and mixing them until every piece was marinated. A few days later the villagers would scoop the turnips into bamboo baskets and set them out in Grandpa's front yard to dry in the sun. Salty liquid dripped from the baskets onto the ground. That is what gave his yard its whitish color and kept anything from growing in it.

After the turnips dried, they turned to a deep brown color. Then Grandpa would package them in plastic bags and sell them.

People—especially the Chinese—ate salty preserved turnip with rice porridge for breakfast. That is most of what I remember of the province of Tekvil, because when I was five years old, my family and I had to leave unexpectedly.

One evening my dad came home and said to my mother, "Say Guech, we have to leave Tekvil tonight." He said that there were riots and that a political revolution was taking place in Phnom Penh, and we must leave town to go stay with Uncle Hak for a few weeks until things calmed down. I thought we were already living in the country, because the province of Tekvil didn't have electricity, running water or indoor restrooms. I couldn't believe that there was a place less civilized than Tekvil.

That evening we packed our family into the back of my father's three-wheeled cart, which was pulled by his Yamaha motorcycle. There were six of us packed together like sardines in a tiny can— Mom, my few-week-old baby sister Heang Ly, my big brother Cheang, myself, my little brother Meng, and Mom's younger sister, Aunt Houy. We also had clothes and a few other belongings packed with us. Grandfather said that it would be best for Aunt Houy, who was fifteen years old, to come along to help Mom with the children.

The Cambodian people believe that women must be bedridden for at least three months after giving birth. They call this period of time "young nerve". During this time a young mother must stay in bed all the time. She cannot walk around at all. Her meals are brought to her, and they have to be specially prepared. Everything she eats and drinks has to be warm; she is given no cold salad or cold water. Most of her food is spiced with a lot of black pepper and ginger root. Her bed is constantly kept warm by coals burning beneath it. Cambodians believe that these practices help a young mother's health to improve more quickly and keep her from getting what they call "reaction to childbirth", which can be deadly. They also believe that strictly following this regimen will give them better control of their bladder when they get old. My mom was not supposed to be out of bed at all. But the desperate situation forced her out of bed. That is why my Grandpa asked my aunt to come and help Mom.

Off we went through the countryside, to a town called Krang Yao. There were no paved roads there. Uncle Hak's house was built on stilts. It was a farmhouse with chickens roaming everywhere, along with hogs and cows. There I learned how to trap chickens. I took a cage made of bamboo sticks and propped it halfway open with a stick, which had a long string tied to it. Underneath the cage we placed bait in the form of rice and yellow corn kernels. When the chickens came in underneath the cages, I pulled the string, and the cage came down and trapped the chicken. My brothers and I played with the trapped hens, and after a while we released them. Little did I know that the leaders of Cambodia's government were playing a similar game with the Cambodian people.

CHAPTER 2

Political Games

Cambodia's government was deceiving us. Later I learned that the riot in Phnom Penh was mostly a political game. While King Norodom Sihanouk was on business outside the country, the American government helped Lon Nol, general of the Cambodian Army, to lead a coup against the king. The riot was an attempt by the new government to chase all the Vietnamese who were living in Cambodia back to their own country.

The Cambodians and the Vietnamese had had a long history of war. Bitterness against the Vietnamese was in our blood. As a child I heard a story about how, long ago, during a war, the Vietnamese captured some Cambodian soldiers. The Vietnamese were merciless and cruel. They dug a hole deep enough to bury three men up to their necks. Then they used the three heads as "stones" to support their kettle while they made hot tea. With history the Cambodian people did not have good relationship with the Vietnamese.

Also we did not want to get involved with the Vietnam War. Cambodia was supposed to be neutral. However we were pulled into the war when the North Vietnamese crossed our border and attacked South Vietnam and the Americans from bases in Cambodia. The Americans warned the king several times to keep the North Vietnamese from using Cambodia as base from which to launch attacks, but he did not comply. That is why the United States helped General Lon Nol in his coup against the king. We did not realize it then, but this act fueled the flame of civil war within Cambodia.

While the coup was taking place, a group of revolutionary Marxist guerrilla fighters, known as Khmer Rouge (French for "Red Cambodian"), was hiding out in the jungle. This group was composed of people who were tired of foreign influence, and farmers who were oppressed by the land-owners, and business-owners. Their leader's name was Pol Pot. Soon after the coup he announced, "All countrymen who are patriotic and love freedom must join the revolutionary freedom fighters in the jungle." Disagreements between Pol Pot's Khmer Rouge and Lon Nol's new government divided the country.

When the civil war began, people left the cities and towns and went into the jungle. It was then that my father thought it was not safe for us to live in town. One reason why we had to move was hatred against the Vietnamese in Cambodia. Since our family had Chinese ancestors, we looked like Vietnamese, and Dad thought that people might mistake us for Vietnamese and harm us. It was reported that some Vietnamese were killed during the riot.

Most people in the country at that time had the misconception that King Sihanouk was the leader of the Khmer Rouge and that one day he would return to reign over his country. (The King was very popular among the Cambodian people, because he had helped Cambodia gain its independence from France in 1953.) On the basis of this misconception, many Cambodians supported the Khmer Rouge. Also the Khmer Rouge made this promise to us, and we believed it: "If we can defeat Lon Nol and establish a new regime, every Cambodian will be free and equal; there would be no rich and no poor. It will be a perfect society." The thought of being free and equal, with no rich and no poor, was very appealing to the Cambodian people. The majority of them were uneducated, illiterate and poor. But even some educated people—teachers and professors—bought into the idea. The Khmer Rouge became very powerful.

What started out as a temporary stay at Uncle Hak's house became longer than we expected. Cambodia was in chaos. My dad thought it was best that we move even farther away from the capital. Late one evening he said, "Boys, your mother and I have decided that it would be better for us to stay with my mom and dad for a while. When things get better, we will go back home. We will leave your mother, Aunt Houy and your little sister here with Uncle Hak. I'll take you three boys there and come back to get them. We will take the boat. It is safer."

That evening we left Krang Yao in a small fishing boat, about the size of a canoe. When we came to the boat, the man whom Father had hired as a guide was sitting in the back of the boat and holding an oar in his hand. He was ready to go. My big brother Cheang, my little brother Meng and I sat in the middle. Dad sat in the front. None of us had a life jacket on. None of us boys knew how to swim. The edge of the boat was just a few inches from the water. I was thinking that if there were large waves in the lake, we might sink.

Soon after we left the shore, a rainstorm began pouring sheets of water down on us. It was unusual to have rain in the summer. (Cambodia has two seasons, the rainy season and the summer season, and this was summer; rain was not expected).

We headed across a lake that was named, simply, "Lake Five Hundred". It was one of the biggest lakes my family had ever crossed. To my six-year-old eyes it looked enormous. The rain poured down, the wind blew, and the waves shook our boat from side to side. The guide yelled to my father, "Sreng, start to bail the water out of the boat!" Then he yelled to us, "Boys, hang on! You can bail the water out, too." Cheang found a half of a coconut shell and began scooping water from the boat and emptying it into the lake. With my right hand I held on to my three-year-old brother, Meng, and with my left bailed water. The guide was using his oar to guide the boat from one wave to the next. It seemed that the waves were much bigger than the boat. But somehow our family made it safely to shore.

Of course we were soaking wet and cold. After we got off the boat, Dad took us to a farmer's house. There we were invited to come in and get dry. I was so happy to see a place with a roof and a warm fire—and warm soup! The farmer's wife washed our clothes and dried them on the furniture around the fireplace.

Before dawn the next morning my father woke us boys up. "Up! Get up, my boys! It's time to leave." We hesitated to get up, but Dad shook us to awaken us. Before the rooster crowed or the first light appeared, we left the farmer's house. Dad wanted to take advantage of the coolness of the morning. Soon enough the sun would heat up the ground, and our feet would feel as though they were burning. None of us wore shoes. We did not know what a shoe was.

Summers in Cambodia were hot and humid. The temperature often rose to 100 degrees, and the humidity made the air feel hot and sticky. Men wore shorts and short-sleeved nylon shirts and seldom wore underwear. Children normally wore only shorts. Boys ran naked until they were five or six years old. The unusual rain of the day before—the "curse" that struck us while we were on the lake—became a blessing. It cooled the ground and made it more comfortable for our bare feet.

Carrying his three-year-old son Meng in his arms, Dad led the way. At first it was too dark for me to see where we were going, and we just followed Dad's footsteps. When dawn came, I realized that we were walking on a dike in a rice field. (Dikes are manmade irrigation dams made of dirt. They vary in size from two to three feet wide and from one to three feet tall. Dikes divide a rice field into squares, making it look like a checkerboard.) It was May, and the rice field had been harvested already. In the field there were golden stubs about knee high. For miles I could see the golden field stretched out as if it would never end. It seemed that the sky came down and touched the field. But as we walked on, the sky seemed to rise, and we never reached it. We walked a whole day before we arrived in Samrong Yong Takeo, the town where my father was born and raised. Our grandparents were not expecting us. We had no way to tell them that we were coming.

I always enjoyed coming to see Dad's parents. They were so kind. Any grandchild would love to have such grandparents. I called Grandpa, "A-Kong". (It is a Chinese word that means "grandfather".) He was a jolly, easygoing, happy man. He and his brother had escaped from China (as had my mother's father) before the Mao Tse Tung revolution and had come to settle in Cambodia. Later he married a Cambodian girl—my grandmother—and settled in this town called Samrong Yong, in the province of Takeo. Together they had seven children—five boys and two girls. My father was the oldest. Grandfather spoke Chinese fluently, and broken Khmer, which is the Cambodian language. Grandmother spoke fluently in both Chinese and Khmer, as did my brothers and I.

My grandfather's family was a very successful business family, and they had a beautiful house—the biggest house in town. It was made of stone and had whitewashed columns in the front. (In Cambodia at that time most people lived in thatched huts made of grass. If people had a concrete house with a tile roof, they were considered wealthy.) Next to the house was a big warehouse where business took place. They had a rice mill—the only mechanical rice mill in town. In this warehouse were hundreds of brown bags of rice brought by farmers to be milled. I spent many days in the warehouse, watching with great wonder as the golden rice grain went into the mill and came out as white rice. The chaff was separated from the rice and blown into a pile. My brother and I liked to jump up and down on it. The warehouse was also our favorite spot for playing hide and seek with my brothers and uncles and aunts. We played outside a lot, too.

Near the entrance to the property stood two magnolia trees. One tree produced white flowers, the other cream-colored flowers. They gave off a beautiful fragrance. A little farther from the entrance stood a long row of mango trees. (I loved to eat green mangos with red pepper and salt.) At the end of the mango trees, close to the road, there was a big water well with a concrete floor around it. A bucket and rope were used to draw the water. A-Kong owned the well, but all the people in the community were allowed to use it freely.

Behind A-Kong's house were two large ponds in which all sorts of tropical fish lived. Water lilies blossomed all year. Big trees, lush green plants and flowers like those that surrounded the Buddhist temple grew around the ponds. Banana, palm, coconut and orange trees grew everywhere. Beyond the ponds were hundreds of acres of rice fields. There was a great contrast between this place and that of my maternal grandparents, whose land grew nothing.

CHAPTER 3

My First Taste of War

The day after we arrived at A-Kong's place, Dad left us to get the rest of our family. Several days later he returned with Mom, our baby sister Heang Ly and Aunt Houy. "A terrible thing happened on the way," Mom said. I will never forget the story she told. They had crossed Lake Five Hundred and were walking along the same route we had taken earlier. "About halfway through the trek," Mom said, "They started shooting from everywhere. Bullets and shells and grenades exploded around us. We were caught in the battle. We tore our clothes and our knees and elbows as we ran and crawled. It was horrible. I thought we would not live through it."

Dad explained that the Khmer Rouge platoons were crossing the field to go somewhere when Lon Nol's platoon started to shoot at them. He said that the Khmer Rouge wore uniforms that looked like black pajamas, and they each had a red scarf, which we called a "krama", around their neck. Lon Nol's platoon wore green camouflage army uniforms and steel helmets. "But the battle didn't last very long," he said, "We lay down by the dike for protection until the shooting stopped. Then we completed our trek." War fascinated me. I wanted to see one.

The riots in town calmed down. We stayed at our grandparents' house for a few weeks. Then Dad found us a house to rent, somewhat closer to the city of Phnom Penh. (My father was a very independent man, and staying a long time with his parents was not to his liking.)

The Khmer Rouge membership increased tremendously. In only a few months they were able to train and assemble a force big enough to start attacking some of the major towns along the borders. Their force consisted mostly of young girls and boys and farmers. By this time they had already invaded and captured my home town of Kendal. "We cannot go back," said Dad. "We have to move toward the capital of Cambodia." So our family moved to a town named Prek A Tang where we stayed for a considerable time.

I was seven years old when I had a personal experience with war. There is a saying among the Cambodian people, "When the elephants are fighting, the ants are dying." This statement is true. War kills and steals. It destroys people. I was walking home from school one afternoon when I saw all kinds of army trucks loaded with soldiers come into town. In the front of the line were several jeeps filled with soldiers who were wearing uniforms and had green steel helmets on their heads. They wore holsters with pistols in them. All the vehicles were painted dark olive green. All the other soldiers in the big trucks had long rifles. One truck pulled a trailer behind it that looked like a big tank for carrying fuel and water. Another truck pulled a large gun on wheels. Later I found out that this gun was used to shoot airplanes down. Then there were even bigger guns, called shell launchers. They were pulled by tanks.

Later that day two soldiers walked from house to house, warning people to stay inside their houses and to take cover, because an invasion by the Khmer Rouge was expected that night. They told us, "Lie down low on the floor with heavy objects around you to protect you when you hear shooting outside." They told my parents, "Make sure your chest does not touch the ground. This will prevent your internal organs from being damaged." To protect us from bullets Dad stacked rice bags on top of each other to make a circular wall, and we stayed in the middle, waiting.

The town was so quiet that day. It was like the calm before a storm; there was no sound of vehicles on the street. The only sound was the barking of dogs. We waited patiently, and listened carefully. I had never seen a gunfight, so this event was quite exciting. I was anxious to see what would happen.

The soldiers dug foxholes along the street. Some piled up sand bags to make protective walls around them. They set up ambushes, like hunters preparing to hunt prey. Then they waited behind their machine guns.

Suddenly the explosions started. They were rapid and very loud. Once in a while a big gun fired. Because our house had metal walls and roof, the sound was deafening. Outside men were running and yelling, "Here they are! Shoot them!" The sounds of running feet and voices yelling and crying were mixed with the explosions of weapons. "Stay down low!" Father commanded. "Keep your head down!" He pushed my head down with his big hand. The fight lasted several hours, and then the shooting died down. For a while there were some single shots here and there. Then the shooting stopped.

People was screaming and crying outside. We could not understand what they were saying. But soon we went outside and looked. People were gathered in front of the next-door neighbor's house. They had formed a circle and were looking at someone who had been shot. Because of my small stature, I couldn't press in to see. But when a jeep with a red cross on it stopped, and some men got out, the crowd moved apart and made way for them. It was only then that I realized it was my neighbor's youngest son that had been shot. He was sitting on the floor, screaming. Both of his legs were attached only with skin and a few pieces of muscle below his knees. Blood spewed out on the ground everywhere. A piece of bone with whitish cartilage stuck out of his flesh. He was screaming in agony, "Mom, help me! Dad, help me! I am in pain! God, please help! Any kind of gods, please help!"

Most Cambodians are Buddhists. They are polytheistic; they believe in many gods. We also believed in a god that will reward good deeds with blessing and bad deeds with cursing. We believed that our suffering in this life might be the result of our actions in a previous life. We thought that if we continued to hold onto the sacred law of the gods, our lives would be better each time we were reincarnated. We believed that maybe—and only maybe—one day we might become like the gods or the angels.

I know now that this is not what the Bible teaches us. But at that time I didn't know what the Bible was. As I was growing up, I had no choice but to embrace the traditional beliefs that my parents and community believed. I didn't know that the Bible is the inspired Word of God. But Pheng, my next-door friend, was calling for a god to help. Had he known the real God; he would have called to Him for help.

As blood dripped from both of Pheng's legs, the soldiers lifted him onto a stretcher and placed him into the Red Cross jeep. They said that the bullet that had amputated Pheng's legs was Soviet-made. They said that it had a double or possibly triple explosive head. One of the men traced the path of the bullet before it hit Pheng's legs. He said that the bullet first hit the magnolia tree in front of the house and exploded there, cutting the tree down. Then the bullet hit the front door and exploded again. There I could see a hole the size of a grapefruit in the front door. Then the bullet traveled low and hit Pheng's legs while he was lying down under a bed.

As the American Red Cross trucks pulled away out onto the street, the driver shouted to Pheng's dad that he would take Pheng to a Russian hospital in Phnom Penh. "If you want, you can find him there," he said. How strange it seemed that the same country that created and sent the destructive weapon which destroyed a Cambodian boy's legs had a hospital to care for its victims.

As I stood there watching Pheng being taken away that day, somehow a dream was permanently formed in my heart. I thought hard about what I was to become when I grew up, and at that moment my future was determined: I would become a doctor, so that I could take care of sick and afflicted people like Pheng. Watching the man from the American Red Cross helping Pheng had fascinated me.

A few days after Pheng was taken to the hospital, we heard that both of his legs were so damaged that the doctor had to amputate them. He would never walk again. He would have to stay in a wheelchair for the rest of his life. Pheng didn't come back home. His family moved to the city to stay with him.

The same war that destroyed my friend's legs also robbed my grandparents of their dream. The Khmer Rouge's power gained momentum after this war, and they took control of most of the country. They forced the villagers to take refuge in the suburbs and in the city. My grandparents and uncles and aunt had to move out of their home, because the Khmer Rouge invaded their home town shortly after Pheng's incident. They came to stay with us for a while, but because our house was too small, they moved into Phnom Penh and rented a house.

I am sure that Grandfather was upset about the moving. After all, he had escaped China to find peace, tranquility and freedom. He had worked hard to get what he had. He came to Cambodia without anything but what he wore on his body. Now, because of war, he was forced to leave behind everything he had and move into the crowded and dirty city. He tried to maintain a good attitude. He said it was only a temporary move and that after the war he would go back to his home and things would be back to normal. Yet he spoke with reservation.

CHAPTER 4

Life near the Capitol

By 1973 Phnom Penh became very crowded. It was difficult to find a home to rent or buy. Inflation became very high, and the shooting became intense. Most of the towns surrounding the capital city were invaded and taken by the Khmer Rouge. The Khmer Rouge's forces took over the country like a wildfire. My family also moved to the city . Dad rented a downstairs room in a two-story house. We lived in a suburb of the capital, called Prek A Tang.

Immediately after we moved there, Cheang and I were enrolled in public school. I was in the first grade, and Cheang was in the third. School started at 8:30 AM and ended at 2:00 PM. We walked about three miles to go to school. Mom and Aunt Houy stayed at home and took care of Meng and Ly Heang. Dad went to work. Since the unemployment rate was so high, people had to do anything to survive. Dad left home early in the morning and came home late at night. He worked as a sort of taxi driver. But instead of driving a car, he drove a motorcycle with a three-wheeled trailer pulled behind it. He transported people, goods—anything. Sometimes our whole family got to ride in it. I remember going as a family to see a movie called "The Horse Head Youth."

What I didn't understand about this war was that Cambodians were killing Cambodians. Without military uniforms, they all looked alike. A man could be a Khmer Rouge, but if he wore civilian clothes, he could go anywhere in the country. People would go to visit the countryside where the Khmer Rouge had control and suffer no consequences. My grandparents paid several visits to their home town and had no problems. People believed that when the war was over, the country would be peaceful and prosperous again, and they didn't mind the temporary inconveniences.

But by the middle of 1973 restrictions were occurring everywhere. The area controlled by the Communists was restricted. If people went to the Khmer Rouge's territory, they were not allowed to return. Yet the Khmer Rouge soldiers, dressed as civilians, came into the towns to bomb public places such as movie theaters, and even schools.

One day Mom received news in a letter from her dad that he was very sick and was not expected to live. In his letter Grandpa asked if Aunt Houy could come back home. He wanted to see her one last time before he died. He said Uncle Sroy had made special arrangements to secure her trip back home. As much as she wanted to, Mom couldn't go with her; she had to stay behind and take care of us. And if she went home, she would not be allowed to return. Losing Aunt Houy was a big blow to our family. It left a void in our hearts. Then we received the news that Grandpa had passed away shortly after our aunt arrived. A funeral was arranged, but our family could not attend. Full of frustration and sorrow, our hearts wept for the loss of our distant loved one. But losing Aunt Houy and Grandpa was nothing compared to what happened to us next.

One afternoon as my big brother and I were playing in the front yard, my dad's parents came, riding in a motorcycle trailer similar to the one my dad operated. That was unusual, because earlier that morning they had ridden in my dad's vehicle. Grandmother was crying as she walked hurriedly, looking for my mother. "Grandma! Grandpa!" Cheang and I called out to them.

"Where is your mother? Take us to her!" said grandmother, wiping her tear-filled eyes with her hand.

"Yes, Grandmother, Mom is inside the house," we said. As soon as we entered the house grandmother called out for my mom, "Say Guech! Say Guech!" Grandmother had never called Mom by her name. She had always called her "Sweetheart".

Immediately mother knew there was something wrong. She said, "Ma and Pa, what is going on?" Grandpa didn't talk. (My father was also a quiet man like his father. When he did talk, people listened carefully to what he said.) Grandpa almost always spoke in Chinese. He could speak Cambodian, but with a heavy accent.

"Your husband, Ngoun Sreng—he has been abducted by the Khmer Rouge," Grandma spoke haltingly.

"No!" Mom exclaimed in disbelief. She started crying. The children gathered around her and started crying, too. Cheang and I understood what was going on, but our little brother and sister couldn't.

"I am so sorry, my sweet," Grandmother said. "This morning your husband took us to see my house. We thought it would be safe. He dropped your father and me off at our old home. He told me that he was going to visit his friend down further. It was then that the Khmer Rouge abducted him into the jungle. We don't know what they are going to do with him. A few people who were also abducted with him escaped, and they told me that your husband could not escape. He was left behind."

"Mom? What are we going to do?" Mom pressed my grandmother for an answer.

"Only wait and see dear," she said.

Grandpa added, "We will send people out to look for him until we find him." I was confused about why the Khmer Rouge would need to take our father away. I thought that the Khmer Rouge were good, patriotic people. My anger started to build up pressure like water boiling in a kettle.

Mom composed herself and said, "Children, we have bad news. Your father is going to be gone for a while. He was taken away by the Khmer Rouge into the jungle. We need to pray for his safe return. We don't know when, but we will see him soon." My grandparents stayed with us for the rest of the day.

That night, before bed, the whole family knelt down on the floor. With incense sticks held in our hands we prayed. I didn't know who or what to pray to, because I didn't know who God really was. Mom prayed out loud. Her prayer went like this: "Dear gods of heaven, gods of earth, gods of fire and gods of waters, the angels, the demons and the spirits of our ancestors, please help my husband to escape from the Khmer Rouge. Keep him alive, please. Protect him and care for him. Don't let them harm a single hair on his head." After Mom finished her prayer, we lifted our incense sticks three times before we placed them into a can. And then we went to bed. Oh, how I wish I had known then that there was a true God and that I could pray to Him. That would have brought us some comfort and assurance. But because we lacked the knowledge of God, we had to do what we believed was the truth, and we had a lot of faith in it. This was a devastating time for my mother. The night was very long.

CHAPTER 5

Life without Father

Children are afraid of the dark, and adults are afraid of the unknown. But all fears vanish when we fall asleep. As the sun brings a new dawn for the next day, the loss of our father brought to our lives challenges we had never before considered. Our family did not realize how important our father was to us until he was gone. Father provided security, food, shelter, family identity, love and care. He worked hard night and day and never complained, and I cannot recall that we ever took the time to say, "Thank you Dad."

[A wise man once said, "People do not realize how precious things are until they lose them." This is true. I encourage you who are reading my story to express your gratitude to your parents while they are with you. Thank them for all the things they have done for you—the little things and the big things. We need to treasure the time we have with our parents, because there will be a time when our loved ones are no longer around.]

The next morning my mother got up extremely early. I wondered if she had slept at all that night. She got me out of bed and said, "Heng! We are going to ask people about your father." We took a three-wheeled motorcycle cart to the market. Mom held my hand tight in hers and dragged me through the busy market. "Sir! Have you heard whether any people have escaped from the jungle? Older sister, did you hear anything about men being abducted by the Khmer Rouge?" Mom stopped every person she met at the market. The answer was always the same: "No." Each time she heard this Mom walked faster to ask another person. We spent all day asking people, but the answers were still all the same. Each answer was a painful blow to our hearts. At the end of the day we returned home.

During the next several weeks, each time there was news of people escaping from the jungle, Mom would be there to ask them if they have seen our father. But the answer was always the same, "No, we have not seen your husband." For several weeks there was no news, absolutely no news. We didn't know whether Dad was dead or alive.

Having no news made it worse. Mom was determined to find out what had happened to Dad. Out of deep desperation she looked in the direction of a fortune-teller for an answer. She took me with her. (It seemed that Mom always dragged me everywhere she went.) The fortune-teller's house was only a short distance away. I had gone there before and picked tangerines from the trees in the front yard. I didn't know that the old woman who lived there was a fortune-teller. After Mom told me that the fortune-teller lived there, I was afraid to even walk across her land. I stood as close to my mother as I could while she knocked on the woman's door. When the door opened, I expected to see a witch coming out, but instead I saw a woman with short gray hair and a gentle and kind face. She gave us a warm, welcoming smile and said, "Come in, come in. What can I do for you, my dear?" She reminded me of my father's mom.

Mom said, "Are you the fortune-teller? I need your help. My husband was abducted by the Khmer Rouge and taken into the jungle. I need to know what happened to him. Can you tell me where my husband is, and whether he is dead or alive?"

"Sure," said the woman. "But it will cost you some money."

"We can pay you. Just please tell me where my husband is," Mom begged her.

Without hesitation the fortune-teller led us to a room that was half filled with all kinds of Buddhist statues—some standing, some sitting. She knelt down in front of one of the statues, brought her palms together, raised them up and began murmuring some words that did not make any sense to me. She brought her palms down and bowed her body to the floor three times. Then she placed a white scarf across her shoulder, with one end across her chest and the other across her back. She took three sticks of incense from a package and lit them with a lighter. With the incense pressed between her palms, she started to pray in a language that I could not understand. She placed the burnt incense in a pot that was full of other burned incense sticks, then laid her head against a big white pillow next to the wall and closed her eyes. After a few minutes she woke up. Her eyes were wide open, and she spoke in a little child's voice. She appeared to be posessed by an evil spirit. I thought it was spooky. I wondered if she knew that I had stolen tangerines from her tree. But she didn't say anything about that. She asked Mom, "What can I do for you?" And Mom said, "I want you to tell me where my husband is and if he is dead or alive."

The fortuneteller leaned her head against the big pillow again, closed her eyes, then spoke. "What is your husband's name? And how old is he?" Mom told her that his name was Sreng and that he was about 33 years old and had dark, curly hair.

The child voice said, "I see him. He is located very far away from here. He misses you. But he is alive. He tried to run away from his captors, but he was arrested again." Mom was happy to hear that he was alive. The woman brought us good news, and that is why we called her the fortune-teller. She asked the spirit to tell her exactly where Dad was, but the spirit said he couldn't. "He is too far away, and things are too vague," said the spirit voice. Then the woman laid her head on the pillow and closed her eyes for a few seconds. She woke up, and the spirit had departed from her. She again spoke in a normal voice. Mom paid her, and we left.

After that day Mom was more composed; she didn't go out every day to seek information about Dad. She believed the fortune-teller and told her children that Dad was all right in the jungle, and although he couldn't come to see us now, we could go there to meet him after the war. Another reason why she didn't go out so often is that she was pregnant. She had gained a lot of weight, and her legs were so swollen that she could hardly walk.

Every evening our little sister reminded us to pray for Dad. She would not allow us to go to sleep if we forgot to pray. Without our father, life became very difficult for us. Because so many people moved into the city, jobs became very difficult to find. Inflation got very high. Young people were drafted to fight a war in which they did not believe. One afternoon some young men ran like animals to hide from being caught and drafted by the soldiers. They hid themselves in a pond and breathed through straws. Others hid in the bushes. Bombs exploded frequently in the city, in public places. Our family's financial resources were gone. There was no welfare system to help a desperate "widow" like my mother.

Walking became more difficult for Mom. To get up from her chair she would push herself against her knee, while supporting her back with the other hand. She staggered when she walked. She had a really difficult pregnancy. People normally delivered babies at home with a midwife there to help. If Dad had been around, Mom would have delivered her baby at home. But now she had to go to the Russian hospital in Phnom Penh. She was there for a week and returned home with twin boys. My grandparents came to help us for a short while, but then their visits became fewer and shorter. They had their own family to worry about.

Mom named her youngest son Chanta and the oldest Chanty. (Later we changed Chanty's name to "Thong".) Someone said, "When it rains, it pours." Someone else said, "Troubles come in threes." These sayings were certainly true for us. A week after the twins came home, Chanta developed a serious illness. Because we could not get the medical care he needed, he died. I didn't know what to think about death then. But I remember how sad we were as a family. The really tragic thing was that he did not live long enough for us to have a photo taken. Father would not even know what his son looked like.

Adversity brings people together. You can know who your true friend or family is when you are down in the deepest hole of life and have nothing to give. We did not have any friends on whom to depend. Of all our relatives, only Uncle Khun, a younger brother of my mother, came to our aid. He and the neighbors nailed together a plywood box for Chanta's coffin. Without any formal funeral ceremony our little brother was buried in an unmarked field. Our family grieved.

Uncle Khun was a college student in his early twenties. He was kind and gentle to our family. He was about five foot six—skinny, but well dressed. His eyes were narrow slits, and he wore glasses. Mom said he needed glasses because he spent so much time studying and reading. After the death of our brother he tried to drop by the house as often as he could. Often he came in the evening after school. I could tell that he had not been to his home, because he still had his white shirt and Khaki trousers on. Uncle Khun was studying law at the university.

Until Uncle Khun came, I did not know that anyone in my family was so educated. Most Cambodians never went beyond grade school. Often Mom told me about how she pleaded with her dad to let her to go to school. He told her, "You are a girl. You will be married, have children and stay at home. You don't need school. But a man needs an education to care for his family." To this day Mom regrets not going to school. It might have helped when she was left to fend for herself and five children.

Uncle Khun stayed with a friend of Grandpa's while attending school. Because of his level of education and his fine character, many people wanted to have their daughters married to him. The family with whom Uncle Khun was staying had a daughter named Sim, who unofficially spoke for him. Their marriage was expected after he finished school. I was so glad and proud to have such a caring uncle. He was good to Mom and us children. He became a father figure to us. I looked up to him.

Uncle Khun stressed to us the extreme importance of education. He said, "Education is the key to your future. Without education you will always be someone's slave. Education gives men knowledge. Education frees people from the bondage of ignorance. It gives you wings to soar like an eagle. You must obtain education while you have the opportunity. And the time to get educated is when you are young. Discipline is as important as education itself. Every person must acquire the art of discipline early in life. Discipline and education go hand in hand; they are like twin boys. Always finish what you start. Don't wait until tomorrow. Don't procrastinate." He also advised us to acquire good character and values while we were still teachable.

Soon after Dad was gone, our family was financially broke. We could no longer pay the rent. Our landlady kicked us out. Dad's parents heard about this, so they built us a sheet metal shack beside the river. Many families built there. Our hut had one small room and a dirt floor. In one corner of the house stood a bed made of bamboo. We covered the bamboo strips with a straw mat to make it more bearable for our back. The house had no restroom, no running water, no bathtub. Our whole kitchen consisted of a triangle of three large stones. We used wood for the cooking fire. Outside, next to the entrance, sat a little bench, also made of bamboo strips. And next to it was a 30-gallon clay pot that we used for storing our drinking and cooking water.

We washed our laundry and took our baths in the river, "a crow's flight" (a few hundred feet) below and behind our hut. Most of the time I was in charge of washing the clothes for the whole family—including the dirty diapers. By the time I was eight years old I was responsible enough to cook and take care of my siblings while mother was gone to the market to buy or sell dried fish, sugar or fruit. Thong, the surviving twin, was a good baby. His favorite place to sleep was on my chest. He never cried unless he was very hungry.

We were desperate, but not starving all the time. Uncle Khun taught Cheang and me how to raise a garden along the river. The land there was very fertile. Cheang and I tilled the ground with a hoe. We grew sweet potatoes, cabbage and broccoli. We could only have the garden in the summer, because in the winter the monsoon would cause the river to flood. In that season the river current became very strong. It carried trees and broken houses downstream with it. Not many people dared to swim in the river during this time. Crocodiles lived in the river also. At flood time we could not catch any fish at all.

During the monsoon season the river could swell to as much as a mile wide, but I could still swim across it. Many people had drowned in this river before. If the monsoon was too heavy, and we could not find fish, I would go out into the field with a white 25-pound flour sack on my back and look for toads. They were big, ugly toads with warts on their backs. They looked as big as giant bullfrogs. I put the toads in the sack and brought them home. In the back of the house, on a block of wood, I took a knife and cut off their heads. They usually opened their eyes and raised their front legs as if they were begging me to let them go. Sometimes I felt very sad about it, but I had to provide food for the family, or we wouldn't live. Mom was gone a lot to the market. We had no milk or formula for the baby brother. Mom taught me to cook rice soup for him. I mashed the rice until it became creamy, then warmed it and fed it to the baby.

CHAPTER 6

Desperate Times

By the end of 1973 my family's situation became even more desperate. Inflation went very high. One month it went up to several thousand percent. We had to pull together even closer to survive.

Early each morning, before dawn, the neighbor's rooster crowed, and we got up. Sometimes I wished I could ring that rooster's neck and have him for lunch! We started our morning chores as early as five o'clock in the morning. My big brother Cheang, who was ten years old then, would ride his bike to the bakery a few miles away to pick up freshly baked French bread. He carefully carried it in a box that was strapped to the rear carrier on his bike. Nothing smelled better than warm, fresh-baked French bread! We wanted very much to eat it, but we couldn't. First we had to try to sell the loaves. If we had one or two left over, then we could divide them up among our family. Even the little baby wanted to have his fair share.

Once Cheang arrived home, Mom would separate the French bread loaves into bags. She gave one bag to me and the other one to Cheang. With warm loaves in our bags we would run from house to house, shouting, "Fresh French bread, fresh French bread, still hot and crunchy! If you wait 'till six o'clock, it will be cold! Delicious French bread! Anyone want to buy it?" My competitors—other boys who were also selling bread—would try to out-shout me.

Normally I finished my route by six o'clock. I tried to not sell the last loaf, so that I could bring it home and share it with my family. But sometimes a customer wanted to buy them all, and we had no breakfast. Really, it was better for the family if I sold all the bread. We needed the money.

When we finished our route, my big brother and I got ready to go to school. School was my favorite place. We walked three miles to get to school. Once I was there, I felt at home. I remember what Uncle Khun told me: "Education is the key to getting ahead in the future." And if I wanted to be a doctor, I would have to study hard. My teacher told me that I was his best student in reading and mathematics. Chorus was fun, but I couldn't sing. We always began our school with the national anthem. All the students went out to the school courtyard. Two students were selected to raise the flag. We saluted the flag and sang. Every student had to stand in perfect formation. Anyone who got out of line would receive a spanking when we returned to the classroom.

School was finished by two o'clock in the afternoon. As soon as the bell rang, the students stampeded out. I ran home as fast as I could. By the time I got home, Cheang would usually be there already, because he rode his bike. Sometimes he had already made a trip to the ice cream store and returned with a big load of ice cream in a cooler. Mom would put some of the ice cream into another cooler for me. This was not for us to eat. Carrying the heavy ice chest by means of a strap on my shoulder, and ringing a bell with my free hand, I tried to sell ice cream to other kids. I had to walk through the neighborhood, ringing the bell, until all the ice cream was sold, before I could return home. Sometimes the other kids ridiculed me. They yelled at me, "Ice cream street kid! Don't you have better things to do than to ring that bell every day?" I didn't really mind, because I knew I wouldn't have to do it forever—only until the war ended. Then we could be reunited with Dad, and he would take care of us.

Mom said, "Things will get better." And she also said, "Son, if you work hard while you are young, then when you grow older, you won't have to work so hard. Develop discipline while you are young. It is easier to bend steel than to bend an old habit." I believed her.

Just when we thought things were at their worst, even worse things happened. We didn't have enough food to supply the family. Mom decided that it would be best for me to live with my father's younger brother and his wife. They were newlyweds and had no children. Uncle Srun was a tall, handsome man, who had some of Grandmothers' features. His wife, Aunt Sanglang, was sweet and considerate, but she was what Mom called a "progressive" woman. Aunt Sanglang rode a motorcycle as wildly as a man. Mom said, "Women are not supposed to ride motorcycles like that!"

I went to stay with them, and they took good care of me for three months. But I missed my family so much that I begged them to take me back to my family. I didn't care about having no food to eat, as long as I could be with my mom and my brothers and sister. Sometimes a young boy needs the love and care of his family more than food.

Whenever news came that someone had escaped from the jungle, Mom would seek out the reporter and ask the question, "Have you seen my husband?" The answer was always the same: "No." And each night, before we went to bed, Ly Heang reminded Mom, "Please pray for Pa." If we forgot, she would fuss, and no one could sleep. I began to see more clearly how much our family had taken Father for granted. When he was with us, we hardly had to do anything, but after he was gone, I had to grow up quickly. Each day I was responsible for the family's firewood. As the Khmer Rouge took control of more and more of Cambodia, many people moved into the city. It was hard to find wood for the stove. Sometimes I had to go far away from the city, into the woods—into areas occupied by the Khmer Rouge. I would chop wood with my axe, place all that I could carry on my shoulders and head back home. There was no time for playing with other young people.

Another thing that kept our family even busier was raising a pig to sell for profit. Mom went to the market one day and bought a piglet from a farmer. It squealed at the top of its lungs when we brought it home. We gave our leftovers to the piglet. But we didn't have many leftovers. So most of the time I had to go to the lake, which was several miles away, to cut wild vegetables that grew near the lake. I stuffed them into a big bag and brought them back home.

We cooked them along with rice husks that Mom had bought from the rice mills, and fed the mixture to the piglet. When the pig was a baby, the chore was not difficult, but when it grew to be a couple hundred pounds, it was a challenge to raise her. The pig became our pet. We grew to love her, and could not bear to sell her. We bathed her to keep her clean, and she slept in the house with us. We never sold her. Later I will tell you what happened to her.

CHAPTER 7

More War

By 1974 the war became intense. We hoped that it would be like labor pains—that it would soon give birth to peace. No place in Cambodia was safe. Out in the countryside B-52 airplanes dropped bombs days and night. Some times the bombs dropped so close to where we were living that they shook the ground like an earthquake. Despite the intense efforts of Lon Nol's army, the Khmer Rouge kept advancing. It seemed that there was nothing Lon Nol's army could do to win. Every day his army officers came in trucks, looking through town for young men and women to join the military. High school and college students were chased by the PM—the neighborhood policemen— who were assisting in the conscription. Some young people ran into the jungle and joined the Khmer Rouge forces. People knew that Lon Nol was losing. The young people who were caught and drafted were not trained properly in the art of war before they were shipped out to the battlefront to fight the Khmer Rouge. They were slaughtered like cattle at the hands of a butcher. The people didn't believe in the Cambodian government system any more. Corruption inside Lon Nol's military regime spread like cancer. Soldiers were sent to battle without pay, and they could not support their families. Morale was very low. In every corner of the city soldiers were stealing things. Civilians were sick and tired of war. They wanted the Khmer Rouge to come in and take over so that the king could reign again and make our country prosper. The people wanted peace.

The Khmer Rouge began using their artillery to launch big shells into the city. In school, students were instructed in how to take shelter in case of bomb raids. In the marketplaces, theatres and malls hand grenades and bombs exploded, killing thousands.

A bomb was dropped on one of my uncles while he was on his way to school. "The horror, the horror of war! Why have you tormented me?" These were his last words before he died. Sometimes in the quietness of the night I could hear myself saying the same thing. The pain of war infiltrated through the country, affecting everyone, from the highest, most affluent people to the lowest and most uneducated boy like me.

[I now know the reason why there is war. It exists because of sin. The Bible says that we are living in a sin-cursed world. Since the time when Adam and Eve disobeyed God and chose to follow Satan, the human race has been cursed with suffering.]

In Cambodia people were chasing after possessions and power. They disagreed with one another's political agendas. They chose to go to war. They shed innocent blood. They went into homes and raped the women there. They took our father away from us. We experienced the truth of the Cambodian proverb: the elephants were fighting, and the ants were dying.

With so much uncertainty and insecurity, my mother thought that it would be best if my brother and I stopped attending school and focused on taking care of the family. My dreams of becoming a doctor were shattered. My big brother was in fourth grade, and I was only in my second grade then. Mom assured us that when the war ended we would go back to school again. I adjusted to the idea. Cooking, washing clothes, raising a garden and taking care of my younger brothers and sister and the pig was enough to keep me very busy. After Cheang and I dropped out of school, Mom had more time to work at the market. She sold fish, meat and fruit, and made a little profit.

As more people escaped from the countryside and moved into the city, sanitation problems grew worse. There was no sewage system. People used the river for everything—drinking, washing, cleaning, and a rest room! So the health conditions were not good. Diseases such as dysentery, TB, malaria and Hepatitis A and B were spreading.

Everyone in my family was healthy until one very hot day in the summer of 1974. Ly Heang, my four- year-old sister, was playing outside with her friend. After a while she came into the house, complaining that she was hot. Suddenly she collapsed. Since the roof and walls of our house were made of tin, and we had no air conditioner, the house was even hotter than the outside. So Mom carried Ly Heang outside and laid her on the ground. She placed her palm on Ly Heang's forehead to take her temperature. Immediately she knew that something was wrong. She said to me, "Heng, get a towel. Wet it and bring it to me so I can cool your sister!" I did as she requested and stood watching. The cool towel did not seem to help. Ly Heang's face turned pale, and her lips turned purple. Mom checked her body temperature again and then said, "Heng, help me take her clothes off. Bring me more wet towels." I did what she said. I took a towel from the bag, dipped it into the clay water jar and hurried back to Mom. She patted and wiped Ly Heang's fore-head and face. Ly Heang was still sweating profusely. She was hyperventilating. She did not respond to the treatment and instead got worse. There was no 9-1-1 to call. We had no phone, no doctor, no medicine, nor a car with which to take her to the hospital. On the ground in front of the house, with her little girl dying in her arms, Mom screamed, "Someone help me! Would someone help me? My daughter is dying!"

Immediately the neighbors, mostly women and children, came to her aid. But there was nothing they could do to help.

One old lady said, "We need some ice to cool her down!"

Mom reached inside her blouse, withdrew some money and gave it to me with this command: "Go to the store and fetch me some ice!" We didn't have a refrigerator, and ice was very expensive. I ran to the store as fast as I could, bought a couple pounds of ice cubes and brought them to my mother.

Mom placed some ice on Ly Heang's face and body and rubbed it against her skin to cool her down. Suddenly my only sister took her last breath, closed her eyes and dropped her head back into my mother's arm. My mother shook her and screamed, "Ly Heang!! My daughter, wake up!" Ly Heang did not respond. "Help me! Please, someone help me! My daughter is dead!" I stood in front of my mother, shocked and helpless. Our eyes filled with tears. My heart broke. We sat there crying together, while the neighbors stood around us. Mom was devastated. With her dead daughter in her arms, she cried out in agony. Her exact words were, "Why, God, do you punish me? You took my husband away, and now you take my daughter! What did I do to deserve this?" Ly Heang was buried next to her younger brother in an unmarked grave. There was no funeral procession for her. To this day no one knows what caused my sister's death. The day before, another girl—one of Ly Heang's playmates—had died from the same condition.

Our lives were never the same after Ly Heang passed away. All of us missed our sister—especially at bedtime. She was not there to say to Mom, "Mommy, please can we burn incense and pray that God will protect Daddy?" We missed her laughter. The person who grieved most was my mother. *[She still blames herself for the death of her daughter, and she does not like to talk about our past.]*

Standing there helplessly and watching my sister die without any medical assistance made me even more determined to be a medical doctor when I grew up. I did not want anyone to go through what my family did.

My mother kept saying, "If only I could have done something different, she would have lived. If only I had had the right kind of medicine." I constantly reminded her, "Mom, you did everything you could to save her life. There was nothing more you could have done." I think Mom was too hard on herself. Here she was, just thirty years old, with no husband to help raising four boys, and without any money. She didn't know where the next meal would come from, and there was no help in a country that was deep in civil war. Life was difficult. We struggled to get by, hoping that the evil war would soon end.

CHAPTER 8

Victory for the Khmer Rouge

By 1974 most Cambodians knew that the Khmer Rouge would win the war. Mom said, "We will return to our home town as soon as the war ends. And we will look for your Dad then." Every day I lived for the day war would end.

On April 17th, 1975 Cambodia was "rescued". Like plants dried and scorched in the desert, our family had waited for the rain of peace to bring us back to life. This day was both one of the happiest and one of the saddest days of my life, and in the lives of many Cambodian people. Normally Cambodians celebrated New Years Day on the 13th of April, and it was a great traditional holiday. All of the shops, banks, markets, schools, and government offices would be closed for three days and nights. Old and young people alike got ready for the New Year by cleaning their houses and buying or making traditional clothes. During the whole week before the New Year they worked to prepare food.

Older people celebrated the New Year by going to the Buddhist Temple in their best traditional clothes. At the temple they met with their friends and family and listened to the monks and the high priests reciting prayers in Sanskrit, which no one really understood.

Young people normally celebrated our New Year outside in the temple courtyard with traditional dancing and games. One game they played was "Throwing the Chhoung." The Chhoung was a soft ball made of cloth materials such as cotton or silk, with a cloth handle.

The girls stood a line about twenty-five feet away from a line of boys. The person holding the Chhoung would sing a love song to the girls. When he finished his song, he would throw the Chhoung toward his favorite girl. Whoever caught it would begin singing her song to the boys. And so it went, back and forth. The music, mixed with laughter, would echo across the city all day and on into the night.

But this year it was different. The whole country was waiting for the suffering of war to end. Instead of hearing the traditional music and laughter and the low hum of Sanskrit prayers, we heard guns and bombs and mortar shells. People stayed inside their homes. Bombs exploded like thunder all over the city. In the dark of the night, explosions lit up the sky across the river like fireworks. Several houses were ablaze, and thick columns of smoke curled upward.

A Navy boat came to the riverbank. A soldier jumped onto the shore with the anchor rope in his hand and tied the rope around the tree. He ran up the shore to a little house that was next to mine. For a moment I thought he was my father coming back to us. When he came closer I recognized him. He was the son of the old lady. In full uniform he had come to take his mother away to safety. He said to his mother, "Word is spreading that all foreign ambassadors and their affiliates have left the country already by airplane or helicopter. The Khmer Rouge is coming! The Americans are losing! The Khmer Rouge has won the victory! The Americans are fleeing!"

Early the next day people shouted on the street. Their excitement burst out like the steam from a locomotive. The birth-pains of war finally came to an abrupt end on the night of April 17, 1975.

I was very excited to hear that the war had ended. For several years I had waited for this day. Finally, peace was here! In a way it was a celebration for me, and for the majority of the Cambodian people. We had packed our belongings and were ready to go home.

In the early morning of April 17, 1975 the Khmer Rouge won the war. They came into the capitol of Cambodia in Army jeeps in tanks, on motorcycles and on foot. They all wore black "pajama" uniforms with sleeves rolled up. They carried small pans rolled up in their pant-legs. On their feet they wore black sandals made from car tires. Red scarves were tied around their necks. They carried loaded AK-47's and wore straps containing magazines of ammunition across their back and chest. A few carried bigger guns, which had a bullet about a foot and half long stuck on their muzzle. (Villagers called these weapons "Banana Blossoms". They were tank-killers.) The Khmer Rouge soldiers looked young—as if they were in their teens. All of them had dark skin.

People flooded into the streets like monsoon raindrops to cheer them on. "Victory! Victory for the revolutionary Khmer!" The Khmer Rouge soldiers responded by shooting their guns into the air and waving their guns with red flags tied to the barrel. Even soldiers from Lon Nol's army joined the celebration parade. These two armies had been enemies, fighting like dogs and cats, and now they were cheering together. I thought then that everything was going to be all right. I felt very peaceful about it. I ran over to the street and joined with the celebration by shouting, "Victory for the revolutionary Khmer!!!"

On the street I heard rumors like this one: "Our country is going to be peaceful once again. The king is to come back and reign over our country as before. We will make our country prosperous." I was so happy to hear that news, but most importantly, my family could now return to our home town. And then we could start looking for our father.

When I returned to our house, Uncle Khun was already there with his motorcycle. He had strapped some of his belongings on the back seat. He seemed very concerned about something. He said to me, "Heng, don't roam around! We all need to stay together until we are ready to go. We don't want to leave anyone behind, do we?"

"No, Uncle," I responded.

Sure enough, late that morning two Khmer Rouge soldiers knocked at our door. When we opened it, one of them said, "Mom, Dad, and comrades, Anka asks that you take your family and leave the city at once. The Americans are coming to bomb us. Anka asks you to leave the city for three days. Once the city is safe, you can return if you choose to." I was confused and happy at the same time. First, why did these two soldiers call my mother "Mom" and my

Uncle "Father"? Why did he call us children "comrades"? And who was "Anka"?

Without hesitation we gathered all we could carry and left the house. Mom insisted that we bring our pig with us. My big brother led her by a leash around her neck.

The street was full of people who were making an exodus into the countryside as we were. After only a few hours the crowd became very thick, rubbing shoulder against shoulder. Our family tried to stay as close together as possible. But the pig was confused and frightened. It screeched and oinked and did not want to follow us. The Khmer Rouge took care of that problem. They pointed guns at us and said, "Anka needs that pig. You don't." They grabbed the leash out of Cheang's hand and led our pet away. One of them beat the pig with his AK-47 to make it move forward. We all were upset about it, but there was nothing we could do. We had to concentrate on one thing—staying together and not losing each other in this enormous exodus.

Uncle Khun walked his motorcycle with Thong, my youngest brother on the seat. Some people carried their belongings on their backs, while others held things on their heads. Some carried children in their arms. Others carried their belongings in wheelbarrows. A man and a woman were pushing an old man on a bed that had wheels beneath it. To my amazement some people even carried TV's. I thought such people had no common sense. What would they do with TV in the jungle when they got hungry? Some people put their loads in a car and pushed it along with the crowd. I had never seen so many people!

Along the street stood Khmer Rouge soldiers, who were yelling, "Get out of the city quickly! Mothers, fathers, brothers and sisters, the Americans are coming to bomb us!" People stampeded. Because of the congestion, we could not walk very far at all. By late that evening we had gotten only as far as the outskirts of town. Uncle Khun said that we needed to camp and rest for the night. Then we could get up very early in the morning and get on our way before the sun heated up the street and burned our feet.

I remember sleeping in the field along the highway that night. I used a big rock as a pillow. I gazed into the sky and for the first time noticed the bright stars and the moon. One can see these things better on a very dark night. I thought how excited I would be to see my Dad again. And at the same time, how sad it would be for him to find out that his only daughter had passed away while he was gone. I also thought about my youngest brother and how that he would never meet my father. Yet thoughts of peace and contentment went through my mind. Somehow I knew that everything would be all right. I didn't know why I was so sure about this happy feeling. Maybe I believed in the rumors a little too much, or maybe the fortuneteller had convinced me.

CHAPTER 9

An Amazing Surprise

At dawn Uncle Khun pulled back my blanket and whispered, "Get up! Heng, get up. It is time to go! We need to get going before it is too hot."

Wasting no time, we got up, packed our blankets and were ready to go. We had no breakfast, and did not brush our teeth. (We never had a toothbrush.) Having no socks or shoes to put on, we walked barefoot. That was why it was important to get started early, before the sun heated up the road, which would bake our feet. Uncle Khun did not have to urge me; I was more than ready to get going. I had hardly slept that night. I was anxious to go back home. I missed my father, and I knew that he would be there waiting for us. I just knew it!

With our personal belongings on our backs, we started our walking marathon of more than 25 miles. It didn't bother me very much to walk, but my mother's feet got blisters, and she began to be in pain. That slowed our walking greatly. On the bright side, it gave me an opportunity to observe the landscape of my country. It had been torn apart by war and left in ruins.

At one time fertile rice fields had lined the road. Now one could see giant holes— craters created by bombs from the B-52's. Palm trees, once green and lush, stood with their tops decapitated. They looked like big black sticks stuck into ground, scorched by fire and discolored by smoke. War had destroyed the people and the country. Hundreds of houses along the road had become piles of charcoal and ashes with grass and weeds growing around them. Each town we passed looked like a ghost town, mostly burned to the ground. Only a few structures stood there to remind us that it was once a town. I felt as though I were walking through an art museum, and that each piece of art hanging on wall was a black and white painting of war and its destruction. "What do you think happened to our home town?" I asked my mother.

She responded, "I don't know son. When we get there we will find out."

We stopped and rested often along the road. So did thousands of other people. Mom said she could not walk any farther. (A few months before, while she was on her way to the market, a motorcycle had run over her right foot and had broken it. Her foot had recovered well enough for her to walk on it, but she frequently needed to rest.) She wanted to rest as long as possible, but each time we sat down, the Khmer Rouge soldiers came and forced us to get up and move on down the road. They said the same polite phrase, "Mother, go quickly. The Americans are going to bomb us." Each time they said that, I was reminded that American bombs were responsible for the destruction of our country. I became more upset. I wondered if the American people knew about the destruction and the horror they had caused with their bombs.

The sun was very hot, and the asphalt street was steaming. It was almost unbearable for soles of my feet to touch it. We had to stop often along the way to rest our scorched feet. "It would have been nice to have a ride in a truck," my mother said.

Just as she finished saying that, a large cargo truck pulled over and stopped beside us. The driver jumped out of his seat and onto the road and shouted at the top of his lungs with both hands around his mouth, "People who are weak, old, or too tired to walk can ride in this truck. Anka will take you to the countryside!"

There was only one truck, but thousands of people. Somehow my mother and I managed to get on it. Mom told Uncle Khun to take care of the rest of my brothers. She said, "We will go home first, and then we will send people with a vehicle to get you!" People were packed into the back of the truck like sardines, standing up, with no air to breathe. Fortunately my mother and I stood at the very back, next to the door.

After a little more than an hour my mother told me we were just a few miles from Kendal, our home town. We were wondering if the driver was going to stop. But then we heard that the driver would not stop at all in our town. He was going to take us as far as he could into the countryside and dump us there. That was his order from Anka.

My mom and I were frantic. We wanted the truck to stop, but there was nothing we could do to stop it. It was like riding on a wild elephant. We couldn't jump, because the truck was going too fast. Panic rose inside me. Then the truck made a sudden stop. The driver needed to use the restroom. He came to the back and told us, "Nobody leaves! Everybody must stay here until I come back."

As soon as he turned to walk away, I jumped down. I tried to be as sneaky as possible, but accidentally I fell flat on my stomach. I was in pain, but there was nothing broken. I tried not to scream. I got up and helped my mother jump off the truck. Then the two of us ran across the street to hide behind the shrubs. When no one was looking, we ran into a house. Inside we saw a man in his fifties. He was startled at first, but immediately his face broke into a smile. He recognized my mother. He said, "Say Guech!"

My mother said, "Yes, Uncle! Help my son and me! We need to hide. Someone is chasing us."

Without hesitation, he said, "Go into my room and stay there until I tell you when to come out." My mother and I did as we were instructed, sitting there quietly, but breathing hard. I could feel my heart beating in my chest as if someone were playing a drum there. It was loud and strange. We were scared. We waited there for a while until Uncle came and got us out. He said, "It is safe now. You can come out. Whoever was looking for you is not here. But your husband, Sreng, was here this morning looking for you."

I couldn't believe the words I had just heard! Happiness flashed into my heart like lightning. No ocean could be deep or wide enough to contain my joy. But the news was such a shock to us that Mother said, in disbelief, "Are you sure, Uncle? Do you mean that my husband is alive and was looking for me?"

"Yes!" he confirmed. "Sreng is living with your older brother, Sroy. He came this morning, looking for you, with a carriage and a yoke of oxen." Mom and I were overwhelmed. Our hearts were flooded with joy, and our eyes were flooded with tears, like water from a broken dam. We embraced each other, crying in disbelief. Finally we could meet our father again! I was so excited. I could hardly wait to see my dad again. I had so much to tell him. How I had longed for this day! On that day our family circle was mended. We were reunited and began our lives together again as a whole family.

That afternoon my father rode on a carriage to meet with us, as Uncle had said. At first we did not believe our eyes when we saw that our father was really alive to meet us. Then we hugged him and cried with him, and after he had held us for a while, we began to believe that what we were experiencing was the truth. That evening Uncle Khun showed up with the rest of our brothers, and our whole family rode on the carriage back to our home town of Kendal.

CHAPTER 10

The Khmer Rouge "Peace"

When we arrived at our home town, Mom asked my father to take us to our home. But Dad said that someone else was living there, and we couldn't ask them to leave. My father learned from neighbors that the Khmer Rouge had held a town meeting and had made these announcements: "From now on everything in Cambodia belongs to Anka. No one can own any property; your houses, your land, your cattle and even your life and children belong to Anka. Now there are no rich or poor. Everyone is equal."

The soldiers told my mom and dad to go and find a place to stay wherever they could. Not knowing where else to go, we camped outside my Uncle's house.

The atmosphere of the town had changed much since we had left five years before. Trees, grasses and weeds were growing wild in town. Houses and other buildings had deteriorated and were damaged. The river, the asphalt street, and the temple were still in their places, but they appeared abandoned and unkempt. The wall of the temple, once decorated with beautiful flowers, was now overrun by grasses and wild bushes. The ground between the road and the temple fence—a place where the neighbors' kids and I once played hide and seek beneath the apple milk trees—had become a cemetery. My father told me that the Khmer Rouge had buried their comrades there—those who were killed in battle. The marketplace had been completely erased; only brown dirt was left there. Our house was still where we left it, but someone else was living in it. "Who lives in our house, Pa?" I asked my father. "Can our family move into our house?" To me it seemed logical that we, as the owners of the house, should live in it.

"We cannot do that, son," he replied with a bitter tone in his voice. "The old villagers have our house, and we will have to find some other place in which to live,"

"But that's our house!" My mother demanded an explanation, her voice tinged with anger.

Dad explained that under the new regime everything in the country belonged to the government. No citizen could own personal property. The government called itself Anka Leu and claimed the authority to make decisions regarding every aspect of our lives. "All the people who just came out of the city—like our family—they call us 'new villagers'. All the people who stayed in the village to help Anka fight the war are called 'old villagers'. Anka gives more privileges to the older villagers."

The "old villagers" were very arrogant about their new status. Most of them had moved into our town from other places. They had been poor, uneducated farmers. One of their new privileges was to rule over us "new villagers".

Along the street, underneath the trees, next to the temple fence, new villagers put up tents. And that is where they had to live. Our father put up a tent next to Uncle Sroy's house, but at night we slept inside the house. Uncle Sroy and his family were considered to be "old villagers". My father said, "Anka has given our house to some-one else. We will have to stay in a tent for a while until they find us another place in which to live. Anka gives priority to the 'old villagers'." Anka provided rations of corn and potatoes. People had to obtain their own meat by fishing in the river.

I was anxious to learn about what had happened to Dad. A few days later, after we had gotten settled, I asked Dad about his abduc-tion. "So, Father, how did you get captured by the Khmer Rouge?" And this is what he told us:

"One day, on the day I took your grandparents to see their home, I dropped them off there and then went farther south to see my friend. He tried to convince me to leave my family and join the revolutionary Khmer Rouge in their fight against the 'Imperialist Americans'—the fight to reclaim our country. He said that Anka (the Khmer Rouge) needed my help to carry food and ammunition to the battle zone. I told him no, but he refused to take "no" for an answer.

"He forced me to go into the jungle with him. There was very little I could do. He and his friends had guns and hand grenades. At least they didn't tie me up or hurt me. We walked deep into the jungle where the Khmer Rouge's camp was and stayed there for the night. That night, when everyone was fast asleep, I sneaked out and tried to run away to come back home. But before I could go anywhere at all, they found me and took me back to the camp.

"They were still nice to me the first time they caught me running. They were trying to indoctrinate me with Communist philosophy. They said, 'Anka has as many eyes as a pineapple, and everything you do Anka sees and knows. Don't run away. Anka needs your help to win the war. And when we win, Anka will reward you for your support. Our feet must destroy the imperialist society. The government of the corrupted system must be burned. The rich are corrupt, and the poor are desperate. In our regime— under Anka—there will be no rich, and there will be no poor. Everyone will be the same. We will start our social and economic life on the same level.'

"I could agree with them on a few ideas, but I didn't want to be with them. They kept a close watch on me, making sure that I didn't try to escape again. For a while they kept me extremely busy. I carried food and ammunition to the battlefields, and then I carried injured soldiers back to the camp. I tried to escape several times, but each time they caught me and tried to indoctrinate me with the same philosophy. After I had made several attempts to escape, they did not trust me anymore.

"After I made one final attempt to run back home, they caught me and tied my hands behind my back and brought me back to the camp. I thought they were going to kill me then, but they didn't. They accused me of being a spy and working for the Americans.

I said, 'No, I just want to go back to be with my wife and kids.' But they didn't believe me. 'Anka does not believe you, Comrade Sreng. You are a CIA agent," they said. I insisted that I was not, but they didn't believe me. Even my friend couldn't help. So they sent me to 'get reformed', but really they sentenced me to die in the bamboo cage. They took me deeper into the jungle, to another of their camps. They put me into a filthy cage, which was already filled with malnourished and sick men. There was no roof over the cage, no wall panels—only frames. Soldiers armed with loaded AK-47's kept vigilant guard over us.

"They gave us nothing to eat or drink. We stayed out in the sun and rain. There was very little I could do in there. After several months my body deteriorated and became wasted. I caught malaria and dysentery. I lived in a pit of human waste, starving. Most of the people there died. I thought I would never see you all again.

"Then your Uncle Sroy found out where I was and came to help me. He brought me some medicines made of opium for the malaria and dysentery. Since he knew some influential people in the Khmer Rouge regime, they released me. But your Uncle had to guarantee them with his own life for mine. He signed a paper, promising them that if I ran away from Uncle Sroy, they would kill him. And that is how he got me released. I came to live with Uncle Sroy and worked on the farm."

Our family owes a debt that we cannot pay to our uncle for rescuing our father. My father was fortunate to have such a brother-in-law who would risk his own life for the sake of another. If Uncle Sroy had not sacrificially helped my father, Dad would never have seen my youngest brother Thong learn how to walk. (Thong started to walk soon after we met our father.) I had no idea that my father had gone through so much. My heart was overwhelmed. I was so happy to see him again.

I learned much from my dad about the influence of friendship. Friendship can shape the course of your life—positively or negatively. It is imperative to have the right kind of friends. Some friends will enhance your life, but some will help you destroy it. And not just one life is affected. Friendship has a ripple effect on many people—husbands, wives, and children. And children feel the consequences most acutely. We can choose our friends, but we can't choose the consequences.

I am reminded of a story about two friends who were walking in the forest. A huge bear began to chase them. One man outran the other and climbed a tree, while the other stumbled and fell to his knees on the ground. The man on the ground panicked. He didn't know what to do—whether to get up and run or stay still. But he remembered an old legend, which said, "If you are chased by a bear and you can't outrun him, just fall down and pretend to be dead." So that was what he did; he pretended to be dead. The bear came over to him, licked him and sniffed around his head and after a few minutes left him and went away. The man in the tree came down to check on his friend and found out that everything was all right. So he asked him, "What did the bear say to you when he licked your ears, friend?"

The man on the ground replied, "You've got one sorry friend. He runs away and doesn't help you in time of trouble." I was glad that my father had a friend such as my Uncle Sroy!

Three days had passed—very quickly, it seemed—since the people had been sent out of the capitol. Everywhere out in the countryside people were putting up tents in which to sleep. At first I didn't understand what all of these new terms, such as "Anka" and "old villagers" meant, but I soon learned. "Anka" means "organization" or "regime". It refers to those who are in charge of other people. The "old villagers" were the people who stayed in their villages during the civil war and helped the Khmer Rouge. People like my father and uncle's family would be considered "old villagers". People from the city—like me—were despised and called "Chinese capitalists" or "new villagers".

The new villagers wanted to return to the cities, but Anka forbade them. Despite all of the soldiers' warnings, no U.S. airplanes ever came and bombed the city. Instead, the Khmer Rouge had a new plan for us. It will be very difficult to describe to you the next four years of my life, but I will do my best.

CHAPTER 11

The New Regime

The Khmer Rouge wasted no time. Only a few days after the exodus they ordered people to work out on the farm. Every capable person had to work. They operated on this principle: "No work, no food." They kept the people extremely busy. Each day my parents got up early and went to work with thousands of other people in the village. Their job was to raise rice crops. They returned home late in the evening, looking exhausted, their bodies covered with dirt and mud. As soon as they got washed up, they were required to attend a town meeting for Communist indoctrination. Most of the time my brothers and I had already fallen asleep before our parents returned from the meetings. They slept a few hours and then had to wake up very early to go back to work.

Each day our family received these rations: two cups of rice and some corn and sweet potatoes. Sometimes we received a small portion of salted pork or fish. Often the ration was not enough, but Uncle Sroy supplied the rest of what we needed. Other people were not so fortunate, because they didn't have relatives like Uncle to help. No one could buy food or anything from anywhere. There were no stores, no schools, no banks, and there was no monetary system. Anka had complete control over us. What they said, we did. The funny thing is I never saw who Anka was. But Anka had the ultimate power. It told people what to eat, when to eat, when to work, what kind of work to do and even where to live.

I never understood why they had meetings every evening. What they said brought fear to my parents. I wanted to know what they were saying in the meetings, and I formed a plan to sneak around and find out about it. But before I could do anything, my parents made plans to send me away to live with Aunt Houy, several miles downriver. By this time Aunt Houy was married to a farmer.

One day, when Aunt Houy and her husband came to visit us, my Mom and Dad called me and said, "Heng, do you want to live with your Aunt? She has more food to eat there than we have here." I hesitated to answer, because I wanted to stay with my family. And I hadn't spent enough time with my father yet.

Dad understood my feelings and said, "Son, it will only be a short while. Besides, your Aunt and Uncle—they don't have any children. You can be a son to them. We don't have enough food here to feed our family. You will do better over there."

"But Pa!" I objected.

Before I could say another word, my Aunt Houy said, "Why don't you try it out? If you don't like it, and you miss your family, you can come back." I decided to give it a try. The next day, early in the morning, I said good-bye to my family and got into a small boat that looked just like the one in which I ridden five years before. This time I had no fear of the river. I knew how to swim.

Aunt Houy was good to me. She and her husband took care of me as if I were their own son. They were an odd-looking couple. Uncle Seang had dark skin, while Aunt Houy had very fair skin. Some villagers commented that this couple looked like a crow holding an egg in its beak! I had plenty of food to eat. We lived on a farm that had all kinds of fruits—mango, jackfruit, coconuts, longan, papaya, pineapples, and pomegranates. Since we lived by the river, we could catch fish, freshwater shrimp, and lobsters. I had never before had so much food to eat. I began to enjoy it there.

One of my responsibilities was to care for the village's cattle. Early each day Aunt Houy packed a lunch for me. She woke me up and handed me my favorite food to take to the field. Along with the villagers' teenagers I helped drive the cattle to the grazing land. Each one of us rode on the back of a cow on the way there and back. Once we got to the pasture I left the cattle to graze and had time to play and learn about farm life. I learned many lessons by living on the farm. One thing I learned about was "taking charge". It was so amazing for me to see that cows and bulls would take commands from me—a person who weighed less than one tenth what they weighed. If I showed them that I had no fear, they ran away or did what I told them. But if I was timid and scared when they charged me, I lost, and they won. Cattle were animals. They were rather dumb.

It was there that my Uncle taught me how to catch fish in the primitive way, without a fishhook and line. We caught them with our hands and feet or with spears, knives and arrows. Also he taught me how to recognize what type of wild plants were edible and which were poisonous.

Three months seemed like a short time, because I was having fun. One day, after I had finished my chores, I came home and found that my parents had come to visit. I was so happy to see them. That evening I cooked dinner for them, using fish I had caught from the river. We had rice with the fish. After dinner we all sat down in a circle, and then Dad told the reason why they had come. "Your mother and I came to take you back with us," He paused, then began again, "Anka has ordered our family to move to Buttambang province, in the far west of our country. It is about 200 kilometers from here."

"We want the family together," Mom added.

"Yes, Mom and Dad," I said. I knew in my heart that, although life was good for me here with my aunt, I would miss my family too much. I decided that it was more important for me to grow up with my brothers than to enjoy life all alone.

The night was long. I stayed up with my aunt and uncle as long as I could. I stayed awake all night, thinking that I didn't really want to leave my uncle and aunt. They were good to me. But I knew where I belonged—with my family. I cried all night. So did my aunt. But we both knew that parting was the best thing to do.

Early the next morning, just before the sun rose, I said goodbye to favorite aunt and uncle and stepped into a little rowboat. After Mom and Dad got into it, we pushed the boat away from the shore and rowed toward Kendal, my home town. We were quiet all the way.

Once we got to the other shore, my parents took me to their new place. They led me toward a two-story house, which I thought must be our home. I was ready to climb the front stairs, when my mother surprised me by saying, "Son! That is not our place. Our place is behind this house." We walked around to our new home. It had once been a barn for cattle, and was only a makeshift thatched building. The roof was made of grasses bundled together with strings. In the daytime sunlight shone through holes in the roof. At night I could see the stars through the holes. *We will get really wet if it rains*, I thought. But the sky was clear, and there was no smell of rain in the air. This was my new home for a few days, until we moved west.

A few weeks after the war, the Khmer Rouge gave this order: "Any man or woman who has been educated beyond high school, all professionals such as teachers, accountants, lawyers, medical doctors, civil servants, policemen or soldiers, and anyone who has had a job with high status must report to Anka. Anka needs you to rebuild our country. We will send you to get the proper training to work with the new regime." Many people believed them and gathered in the middle of town. Some people who were really nothing before the war lied about their identity and joined this crowd, hoping that they would be trained for a better life. Since my mother's brother, Uncle Sroy, was one of the "old villagers", he knew that this could be a plot or trick of the Khmer Rouge to weed out all the people they hated and destroy them. He warned us not to volunteer to go to any school. No one in our family went to this training. Several cargo trucks came to town and picked these people up—supposedly to take them to the training camp. But these people never returned to their families. Rumors spread through the villages that these people had been shipped away like cattle going to the slaughterhouse. The Khmer Rouge dug a big hole in the ground with a bulldozer, backed the trucks up to the hole, dumped the people into the ground and sprayed them with machine gun bullets.

We lived in worse conditions than we had experienced during the war. Even though our family was together, our life was not happy and free. Anka dictated how we would eat, when to sleep, when to work and where to live. We had absolutely no freedom. Everything in the country belonged to Anka. Two nights before we were forced to move to Battambang, the same two trucks that had taken away the elite people came into town with loads of trash from the city. They dumped both loads in the middle of town, beside the road, across from our old home. All the people in town were told to come to these trash piles to see if they could find anything useful. It was like going to a garbage dump. I dug into the middle of the trash, looking for items worth keeping. We had a saying in Cambodia, "One man's trash is another man's treasure."

In the middle of that mountain of trash I found an unusual-looking horn. It did not look like any horn I had seen before. I knew it was not a cow or water buffalo horn. It had red silk wrapped around its base. I wanted my father to see it, so I brought it home. People brought spoons, forks, knifes, cooking utensils, clothes, combs and many strange things to their homes, but I took a horn. "Look what I found at the dump father!" I showed him my new treasure. "What is this for, father?" I showed him the strange object. "Wow!" My father exclaimed with excitement. "My son, this is rhinoceros horn! It is very valuable." I thought, *what is so special and valuable about rhinoceros horn? What can people do with it?* Father told me that it was a very important treasure I had found and that we needed to carefully hide it. Later I will tell you why this horn was so important. I gave it to my father for safekeeping.

While our family was waiting to be transferred to the western province, my new responsibility was to gather food for the family. I was not old enough to join Anka's workforce. During the day, while my parents were away at work, I also left home to gather food for the family. I walked along the creek that led to some swampland, to search for snails, fish, frogs, wild vegetables and eels—anything I could find that was edible. I waded into the swamp until the water reached my neck. I swung a wooden basket in a scooping motion underneath the floating plants. Carefully I raised the basket above the water and began the sorting process. I took plants and trash out of the basket and tossed them back into the water. Then I surveyed the bottom of the basket for minnows, baby crabs, goldfish, snails, and eels. Sometimes I was unlucky and found only trash or sticks in the basket. I learned to be very careful when I stuck my hand in to pick out the trash or sticks. A stick might not be stick at all, but a snake pretending to be a stick! The villagers called these creatures "stick snakes.' They were poisonous. The villagers told me that anyone who was bitten by one of these snakes became sleepy and died. These snakes were everywhere. I was the most scared when a large snake would slither past me, flashing its tongue in and out as if to say, "Get out of here boy, or I am going to kill you!"

By this time I had begun to recognize which snakes were dangerous and which were not. Most of the snakes that live in the water in Cambodia are not poisonous. Water lily snakes, for example, are harmless. They grow to be about three feet long, live in the water and eat fish. I killed them by grabbing their neck and biting their head. Sometimes I would grab one by the tail, swing it in circles above my head and smack its head against a tree-trunk or some other hard object. King cobras, on the other hand, I avoided. But one could not recognize what kind of snake it was until it came close. I assumed that every snake was dangerous until it was dead. I was told that poisonous snakes swim on top of the water, and nonpoisonous snakes swim under the water. The villagers may have told me the truth, but I did not trust them. To me, snakes were snakes.

The Khmer Rouge was like the stick snake. They pretended to be innocent and harmless, but they were deadly. Under cover of night they sent out their investigation teams to eavesdrop on the new villagers' conversations. Using this information, they incriminated civilians, arrested them and tortured them to obtain confessions. And most of the time they killed their suspects. Like snakes, they preyed upon people and killed them at night, while pretending to be gentle and kind during the day. They called the older ladies "Mom" or "Older sister" and the older men, "Father" or Older brother."

They called the young people "Younger brother" or "Younger sister" during the day, but during the night they would kill them.

All the new villagers were anxious about this moving that Anka had planned for us. Some people believed that the trucks might dump us into a hole, where we would be shot by machine guns. We were reluctant to move, but we had no choice.

A convoy of military trucks arrived at our town. Thousands of people were on the street, waiting to be transported. "All the new villagers must go!" was Anka's order. One by one, the members of my family climbed onto the back of the truck. To our surprise, my father's parents and all his brothers and sisters got into the same truck that we had boarded. I did not realize that they, too, had been staying in Kendal. Uncle Khun stayed behind. Anka must have learned about his education and decided to keep him where he was. Mom cried while saying goodbye to her relatives. "I will never see you again," Mom told Uncle Khun.

He tried to comfort her by saying, "Sister, we will see each other again in four or five years at the most. I promise." He seemed to know that this ruthless regime would not survive for long. We wiped away our tears, waved goodbye to our loved ones and headed for an unknown destination.

CHAPTER 12

The Western Province

The trucks hummed through the villages through which we had walked several months earlier. The only view we had was through the opening in the back of the truck. In Phnom Penh there were no people. Streets, homes and buildings were all empty. Trash littered the streets. The city was completely wasted. It looked as if a tornado had come through it. Cars, trucks and motorcycles were left parked at the curbs. Some cars were sitting on concrete blocks. They had no tires, because The Khmer Rouge had used the tires for making sandals. Doors and gates had been left open. Grass and weeds had grown tall and wild. Stray dogs roamed freely, as if they were the masters of this vast domain—dogs that once begged for scraps from a family's table, or were chased away with sticks. The world had turned upside down.

The trucks roared past the Royal College, the place where the privileged and elite students received their education. Pictures of these people came to my mind. I imagined some of them lying dead in a mass grave. I pictured others plowing farmland in the country, with Anka closely watching them. People in the truck were jostling each other, trying to get a glimpse of the city through the opening in the truck cover.

The trucks continued on their course, passing the "Olympic Stadium," a place that spoke of a glorious time in Cambodia's history when Cambodia was at peace and prosperous enough to host the Olympic games. Then we reached edge of town.

Outside Phnom Penh the trucks stopped near the railroad tracks. The driver came back and told us to get out. All along both sides of the railroad track a sea of people sat under the hot sun. They, too, were waiting for the train to take them to ButtamBang. As we talked with them we learned that some of them had already waited for several days. The odor of human waste was very strong. There were no rest rooms, no water and no trees for shade. People used the field for their urination and waste. They were treated worse than cattle being taken to the slaughterhouse. Even the cattle are fed well before they are killed.

After we got off the truck, our family found a place for our bags, and we all sat down. My father's parents and his family sat with us. It was hot, humid and stinking. There was no water to drink or to help cool our bodies. None of us had eaten since early that morning. The sun had no sympathy; it shone brightly. Everyone was in a bad mood. This was especially difficult for my Aunt Keang, my father's youngest sister. She was thirteen years old, and spoiled. As a daughter of a rich parent she had never had to work, nor had she experienced hunger. My grandmother had spoon-fed her until she was almost seven years old. She was not thankful. Everything was, "Mine!" She was immature and undisciplined for a girl of thirteen. She could not handle adversity. She complained about everything and cried all the time. "Mom!" she whined, "It's too hot! My head is burning. I'm starving. I'm thirsty. When are we going?"

Freedom, liberty, and the pursuit of happiness were the things my grandpa sought when he escaped from China and came to Cambodia. He had known what hard times were before he came to Cambodia. So what we were experiencing was not new to him. While we were waiting for the train to come, Grandpa told us the story about how he ran away from China and came to Cambodia.

He left China on a merchant ship that was traveling across the ocean. He said, "We did not have much food to eat while we were in the ocean. Most of the people on that ship ate only one little salted crab with rice porridge each day during the entire trip. We sucked on a tiny crab leg just to taste the flavor of salt." He spoke proudly in his broken Khmer, with his Chinese accent. "To me," he said, "that one tiny crab leg per day was like a drop of rain on a thirsty desert." Then he turned to his spoiled daughter and said, "My daughter, we need to be patient in these desperate times. Crying does not help us at all."

We waited beside the railroad tracks for three long days and nights. We slept out in the open field. My brothers and I played games to see who could count the most stars in the sky. During the daytime we played with the rocks on the railroad track to see who could throw them the farthest. The morale of people was extremely poor. Cambodian people are normally courteous and cordial, but after three days and nights without food and water, anger and bad feelings were expressed loudly. Finally the train came.

None of us knew for certain where the train was going to take us. Some rumors spread that we may be heading to gas chambers like those the Nazis used for killing Jews during World War II. Our life was out of our control. Someone else was deciding our fate. As we stood in the train, holding on to each other and listening to the noise of the train, fear was our companion. Beneath our feet we could hear the "Thub, Thub, Thub," of railroad ties being beaten down by the weight of the railroad cars. It took nearly the whole night for the train to reach Battanbang.

"Battanbang" means "the lost stick". I once heard the story of how this province received its name. A man went into a jungle forest with a big stick in his hand. A stick is very important when one travels in the jungle. A person can use it to protect himself from tigers, wild dogs, wild hogs and snakes. This man went into the forest with his cattle. While he was there, he lost his stick. So he named the place, "Battanbang". Before the war, Battanbang was well known for sweet oranges and beautiful women. Many popular love songs had been written there. In a way I was excited about seeing it. .

The train slowed down and stopped early in the morning. It was still dark when we arrived. The conductors ordered us off the train. We fetched our belongings and walked down along the river. We came to a large crowd of people, who were trying to climb onto the back of cargo trucks. Once the human cargo had been transferred from train to truck, our mysterious journey began again. We did not know where we were going, and it was still too dark for us to see. The truck was crowded. There was not enough room for us to sit, so everybody had to stand. The unpaved road was full of potholes. Several times the trucks had to slow down and move like turtles. Fortunately, it took only a few hours to complete the journey.

The trucks slowed down and pulled into the courtyard of a very large Buddhist temple. In the courtyard there was a big pond. The thought of going swimming came to my mind, but having water to drink was more important. As soon as we got off the truck, Dad found a place for us to camp under the mango trees. I went over to the pond to get drinking water for the family. People swarmed the pond like bees on a honeycomb. People were everywhere in the courtyard.

It was here for the first time since the Khmer Rouge took over Cambodia that I saw and knew who Anka was. On the day of our arrival, in the evening, four men were walking together among the "new villagers". They were average in stature and appeared to be very humble in the way they were talking. The leader was named Hai. He walked in front of everybody and greeted them as he passed by. He was very polite. "Greetings, Mom, Dad, Comrades. How was your trip?"

After he walked through the courtyard inspecting everything, he made an announcement with a hand-held microphone. He said, "Greetings from Anka. We trust that your trip was pleasant enough. We welcome you to Section Four of Battanbang. This village is called Prek Kroche. (In Cambodian this means Orange Creek.) Tomorrow morning the old villagers will come and take you to their places. You will stay with them until Anka gives you further instruction. I am comrade Hai. I am your leader!" With that he and the other three men left the courtyard.

As soon as he left, an emergency developed. A man was found lying on the ground, having a seizure. His teeth were clenched together tightly, and his mouth was full of foam. People stood in a circle around him, watching as he went through the episode. I watched him also. Someone in the crowd shouted, "This man is possessed by a spirit. Is there a priest to cast this evil spirit out of him?"

Another man said, "He is not possessed. He has rabies. Look at his mouth!"

The yelling reached Hai and his troops. Hai came quickly on his bike, with his partners running behind. With his fist he hit the man on the head twice, as hard as he could. Suddenly the man stopped jerking, and his body became still.

Comrade Hai went to his bike, grabbed a rope and tied the man's hands behind his back. By that time the man had regained consciousness and was wondering what had happened. Comrade Hai, with the help of his friends, picked the man up, set him on the bike and walked toward the house. The crowd was stunned. Hai walked the man on his bike until he came to a coconut tree. There he tied the bike and the man to the tree. He left them there all night. Everyone watched in horror. No one dared to release the poor man. His family cried and looked on as helplessly as a gazelle does when one of his friends becomes prey in the jaws of a lion.

The next day the old villagers came. They brought carts pulled by oxen. Our families chose a cart and put all our belongings on it. We climbed aboard, and the man took us to his home. The man was in his fifties, had dark skin and looked very strong. He wore a pair of shorts, but no shirt, leaving his massive upper body exposed. He kept quiet all the way to his home, except to command his oxen. But constantly he wore a little smile on his face. Many ox-carts followed behind his. He drove to a big, beautiful two-story house and stopped there. The house stood on stilts about eight feet high. Around the house there were all kinds of trees—coconut, mango, papaya and orange. At the corner of the house was a small pond that looked like a well. Steep steps led down to the water.

The man stopped his oxen. He got off the cart, tied the reins to the yoke handle and said, "Welcome to my house. Four families can stay downstairs, and one family can stay in the little house behind there. We will use coconut leaves as walls to divide the space downstairs and give your family privacy." He pointed to the pond and said, "That is where you can get water to wash, cook and drink." With that, he walked over to his oxen, released them from the yoke and led them away to eat grass. We all began to unload our belongings. Each family found a corner in which to stay. My grandparents and my family took half of the downstairs. Two other families took the other half.

A few hours after we arrived and unloaded our belongings, Comrade Hai came by with his followers. He was on a bicycle, while his friends were on foot. They all wore black shorts and a shirt and had sandals made of car tires on their feet. They walked from house to house announcing the meeting time. They came over to our family and talked to my parents. "Anka needs you and your wife to come to the town meeting this evening at the town hall located down there," Comrade Hai said, pointing toward the place. He went over to my grandparent's room and said the same thing. Finished, he called to his followers, "Comrades, let's go." His followers were in their early teens. They all had very dark skin and did not smile. Their eyes had a penetrating appearance. Their faces bore an expression of hatred. I found out later that they were spies for Anka.

In the evening the adults met in one place, and young people from junior high age down to seven years old met in another place. Mom and Dad took our baby brother with them. I am not sure where my big brother went. He was thirteen years old, but he looked like a young adult. Cheang always looked big for his age.

I had fun at the meeting. They taught us how to sing new songs. A lady in her twenties stood up with a man about her age and led us in singing a new national anthem. These are the lyrics, as recorded on page 207 of Haing Ngor's book, *A Cambodian Odyssey*:

We are uniting to build splendid democratic Kamphuchea,
A new society with equality and justice,
Firmly applying the line of independence, sovereignty and self-reliance.
Let us resolutely defend our motherland, our sacred soil and glorious revolution!
Long live, long live, long live, democratic, prosperous and new Kamphuchea.

Let us resolutely raise high the red flag of revolution.
Let us build our motherland!
Let us advance her with a great leap forward.
So she will be more glorious and marvelous than ever!"

During the meeting they said, "Welcome, comrade boys and girls. Anka is happy that you have come to be with us. We are one big family. You are my little comrades, and we are your big comrades. Therefore call us 'big comrades' from now on."

The man stood up and said, "My name is comrade Teung. I will also be working with you. Starting in a few days, everyone will be required to attend school." School! I was excited at the sound of "school". I thought I could not wait until school started. Comrade Teung continued his speech: "Now everyone is equal. Nobody is rich, nobody is poor. Anka will take care of you from now on. Your parents have their own responsibility and will not have time to care for you. Anka needs them to work to rebuild our country. No one can own any private property. Everything, including your life, is the property of the state. We are one family. We will eat together when we have food. We will starve together when we have no food." Anka needs you to set an example for your parents." After the indoctrination speech, they brought mango fruit, and we shared it.

Dad left for work in the jungle with most of the men in the village the next day. Anka ordered them to clear the forest and make rice fields. Dad said that it would take a couple days of walking to get there. Mom also left the house early in the morning to work with all of the ladies in town. I was not sure what they were doing, but I am very sure they did not go shopping. My big brother Cheang went to live far away with a group of older youth. That left my two younger brothers and me at home. Meng and Thong were too young to work. They stayed at home with my grandparents. I went to school.

CHAPTER 13

School and Work

Their school was not at all what I expected. It was pure Communistic indoctrination. Early in the morning we met in the courtyard of the abandoned Buddhist temple. After everyone came, the leaders separated the boys from the girls. Then they divided us into smaller groups. A leader was appointed for each group. All the leaders except Comrade Hai were in their early twenties. (Comrade Hai was probably in his thirties.)

After the groups were formed, Comrade Teung took his group to a shady spot beneath a mango tree and began to talk to us. He said, "Under our Anka Communistic regime, we have rules to follow. Anyone caught disobeying the rule will be rewarded with an appropriate punishment." There were many rules, but I remembered these most clearly:

1. No work, no food
2. No stealing
3. No speaking of foreign languages.

During the first few weeks they made working fun. I arrived at the Buddhist Temple around eight o'clock in the morning and attended class for several hours. Then we lined up in single file and marched to the rice field. Out on the farm, they taught us to discern between edible and poisonous plants. We gathered little green plants called "trakoun" and put them into big rattan baskets. When the baskets were full, we brought them into town and took them to the town commune, where we all ate lunch and dinner. On the way to and from work our leader led us in singing new Communistic songs.

The fun time changed to hard work and no play. The Khmer Rouge changed their attitudes like seasons change from summer to winter. As the monsoon season began, Anka forced the people to work harder. They said, "If we work hard now, we will have enough food to eat in the future. Also, we will have new farming equipment to help us."

My parents worked from dawn till dark, and so did I. First Comrade Hai told us young people to build two big ponds by his house. We dug the ponds with hand tools—hoes and buckets. Comrade Hai said, "After the ponds are finished, we will raise fish in them for the villagers' food. As soon as the monsoon season came, fish and ducks were brought to the ponds as he said. But none of us ever enjoyed the fish. They were for Comrade Hai and his "old villagers". We new villagers had no privileges. After a hard day of working, we would meet at the commune for dinner. A big pot full of watery rice porridge and wild plants awaited us. That was what we were given to eat every day for four years.

Every evening I carried a big stainless steel pot to the commune to get my daily ration. I stood in the line among many hundreds of young people, waiting for my turn to receive food. In the summer we stood under the hot sun, and in the monsoon season we stood in the rain. The rice porridge had no taste. No salt, spices nor meat were ever added to that tasteless soup. We ate it only because there was nothing else to eat. All of us went to bed hungry every night.

It was clear that Anka was discriminating against the new villagers. They used fear and starvation to control us. They said that under Anka everybody was equal, but we were not. The "old villagers" had more freedom and—most importantly—more food to eat. They were allowed to have cooking utensils and gardens. They could eat fruits and vegetables from their garden. But we new villagers could not have any food at home. We could eat only what was given to us at the town kitchen. Comrade Hai said, "If Anka catches anyone stealing anything—even just one pepper—you shall surely be put to death. And if Anka catches people holding a meeting without Anka's permission, you will be punished—perhaps by death."

An old Chinese proverb says, "One cannot force a mule to work without grass." But that is what Anka did. Seven days a week, from morning until night, we worked without rest in the rain and under the hot sun. We all wore black clothes. Black absorbs heat from sunlight. It caused people to become dehydrated and to suffer heat strokes. None of us was allowed to wear anything colorful.

Dad was gone to the forest for several months before he came back home. The only reason why he was allowed to come was that he was forced to carry an injured man back to the village. One of the men in his group had accidentally cut his leg with an ax while trying to cut down a tree. Dad and another man were ordered to carry this man on a stretcher for several miles to bring him back to his family. It rained during their trek, and they slipped and slid all over the path. Finally they reached home. My father was a strong, well-built man—bigger than the average Cambodian man. When there was a special job that needed doing, Anka always picked him to do it.

Our family was very happy to see him. When a family is together, even the most desperate times seem more bearable. With Dad back at home, our family was more secure and hopeful. All of us worked hard all day. At night we went out like creatures of the night, looking for food to eat. We knew that the consequence for stealing food was death. And we knew that at night Comrade Hai and his followers spied on us. But we were hungry. We had to do something. If we didn't, we would die.

One night Dad went outside in the rain and stole green bananas from the "old villagers" garden. He boiled the green bananas in a big pot. We ate them secretly, huddled under our mosquito nets. It did not taste good, but it filled us up and gave us some nutrients. The next morning, Thong, my little three-year-old brother bragged to the neighbor's kids. He said, "Last night I ate a banana." He didn't realize that his words would bring dire consequences should Anka hear of them. Fortunately we heard him before his story could spread, and told him to keep quiet.

While the people were out in the field working, Comrade Hai and his spies went from house to house and searched through the new villagers' belongings, checking for documents that would identify who people were, or what kind of occupation they had held before the war. They took with them precious items such as jewelry, watches, gold, diamonds and anything else they thought was of value. Several times after we came back from the field, we found our belongings scattered and misplaced. One afternoon I walked past the spies' compound on my way to work. The spies were still sleeping in their hammocks. The lamp on the wooden table beside their hammock was still lit. The glass reservoir of the lamp was half filled with gold necklaces, rings, diamonds and rubies, all swimming in kerosene. These people had no understanding of the value of precious things. They operated on this philosophy: "To keep is no gain; to let go is no loss." Several times I thought about stealing that lamp. But those precious items meant nothing to me at that time; I needed food and security.

The spies slept during the day and did their work at night. They worked like vampires, sneaking from house to house in the middle of the night, eavesdropping on people's conversations. They tried very hard to walk without making noise, so that they would not be noticed. But sometimes we heard them when they stepped on dead tree branches.

They went into our neighbor's place, pulled the husband and wife out of bed, tied their hands behind their backs and dragged them, while they begged for mercy, out into the darkness. "Please sir!" our neighbors pleaded, "Don't kill me! Sir, my children need us!" Their pleas fell on deaf ears. The spies responded in angry tones, "Don't call us sirs! We are comrades!" They dragged them and beat them as they went. None of the people who were taken away ever returned.

Each night we found it hard to sleep because of the fear that we would be the family they chose for that night. Refusing to die by starvation, I would sneak out in the night to look for food. The spies usually came in the early morning hours. So I sneaked out and tried to be back before they made their rounds. I learned how to catch fish in the dark. I would crawl into the lake like a snake and touch the bottom of the lake with my hands and feet, feeling for any thing that moved. Sometimes I used a line and hooks.

Starvation and sickness forces people to do anything. Most of the new villagers traded what gold and precious stones they had to the old villagers for food and medicines. Gold necklaces and bracelets were exchanged for a few pounds of rice and potatoes. Diamonds and rubies were exchanged for a few antibiotic pills such as penicillin or tetracycline. The trading had to be done in the dark and with secrecy. Mom or Dad had to cook in the dark. When Mom was cooking, Dad and my brother were watching for Comrade Hai and his spies. If we saw them coming, we would put out the fire and hide the food.

One night we traded some gold for rice. We hid it in a special space. That night Comrade Hai called a town meeting. After the meeting we came back home and found that the rice was gone. Our neighbor's wife, who was pregnant and had an excuse to not attend the meeting, stole our food and ate it all. To cover up her plan, she complained to Comrade Hai. She said, "My neighbors are stealing my property." Comrade Hai and his spies came and searched our belonging. Our family was afraid that this woman had set us up by planting some of her things among our belongings. Our whole family would be put to death if they found anything in our place that belonged to her. Fortunately they did not.

As frustrating as this was, we could not do anything about it. A few days later Comrade Hai and his spies took my parents to interrogate them. My brothers and I were very much afraid for their lives. We thought that it was the last time we would see our parents alive.

"Comrade Reth and Seng, did you, or did you not, speak French last night?" Comrade Hai demanded an answer from my parents. "If you tell Anka the truth, we will let you live! If you lie, you will die!" he said.

"No, Comrade Hai," my mother said. "We are Cambodians."

"We don't speak any other language," Dad added.

"But that's not true. Anka heard you speak French," Hai tried to intimidate my parents.

Then my mom confessed, "Oh, Comrade Hai, last night I was in a lot of pain. My eye has an infection. It has an abscess. I told my husband that if I had aspirin, it would help to ease my pain."

"Aspirin is a French word, is it not? Didn't Anka tell you that no foreign language may be spoken?" He demanded agreement.

"Yes, Comrade." Mom and Dad nodded their heads.

"This time Anka forgives you, but next time we will not. Take this piece of medicine. Mix it with the juice of a young coconut put it in your eyes. You can go back to your family," he said.

"Yes, comrade. And thank you." My parents showed him their gratitude.

Mom did not know what the medicine was, but I knew what it was. It was a dried human gallbladder. Each time Comrade Hai took a person out at night to kill them, he kept two things: gallbladders and livers. He put the gallbladders out to dry on a string in front of his house. He had his cook fry the livers, and he ate them. Killing a person to obtain their gallbladder for treating sore eyes seemed like strange medical therapy to me.

I saw other strange medical practices. We used the rhinoceros horn that I had found to treat fever and infection. My father scraped the horn with a piece of broken glass to make a powder. Then he mixed it with water and made me drink it. I believe that it was closer to voodoo than science. It did not work. Before I go on with the story, let me tell you a few more strange medical treatments. This will help you to have a more grateful attitude toward modern medical practices.

Once I developed a high temperature. Mr. Pai, the old villager, told my mother the old village remedy for fever. He said, "Get yourself a green coconut fruit. Go to the back yard, dig in the ground and find some big earthworms. Take some pieces of dry human feces and put them in the cut-open coco shell along with the worms and let them crawl in there for a few hours. Add leaves of "rat's ear" *[a green herb]* to the potion and let the sick boy drink it." When this sick boy heard about that terrible stuff, I ran for my life. I was healed without drinking a drop of it.

My big brother Cheang told me a story about Comrade Hai and the human liver. He said that out on a farm, far away from the village, at lunchtime a woman began complaining about the food. She made a big scene and didn't realize Comrade Hai was coming. She said, "We work hard every day from morning till night. Anka promises equality and good food. But look at the food! Even pigs would not eat it!" She caused an uproar. Comrade Hai and his followers, riding horses, came upon the scene and saw the crowd in disorder. He jumped off his horse, ran over to the woman, took a small wooden hatchet from behind his back and hit her in the back of the skull. She fell to her knees and then onto her face. The wooden hatchet handle broke. The woman went into a seizure, her body thrashing back and forth. Hai ran into the kitchen and came back with a meat-cleaver in his hand. He went over to the woman, kicked her body face down and chopped through her rib cage with the cleaver. He stuck his hand inside her body and pulled her liver out. He raised the liver up above his head. Blood ran down his arm and dripped onto the ground. He screamed at the top of his lungs to that shocked and frightened crowd, "Any one of you who ever complains against Anka will be destroyed!" He took the liver to the kitchen and cooked it, while the woman lay dying. Then he ate it.

After Comrade Hai interrogated my parents, fear was the predominant feeling in our family. At night we were all afraid to go to sleep. Anka's spies walked to different houses. We heard their footsteps. And then we heard the cries of the wives and children begging for mercy for their husbands and fathers. Anka took all the educated people, such as lawyers, doctors, teachers, pharmacists, and people who had any connection with the previous government, and killed them all. My father changed his name from Sreng Sim to Seng Sim to make it sound more Cambodian. My mother also changed her name from Say Guech to Sok Reth. When people asked them what their profession was, they said they were farmers.

We became starving farmers. We did not have enough food. We did not dare to steal. We had no more valuables to trade for rice or fruit. Our family became malnourished. The same was true for my grandparents' family, who lived not far from us. All the new villagers were malnourished. We looked like skeletons. Our knees seemed bigger than our heads.

Sometimes, on really dark nights, I would sneak out into the rice field. (When it rained, the moonlight and the stars disappeared.) I learned to catch fish, snails, crabs and frogs in the dark. I brought them home and cooked them with wild vegetables and fed them to my family. We shared food with my grandparents. We shared almost everything—the pain, the sorrow, but most of all we shared the fear.

As we became starved and knew that we were going to die anyway, fear took second place to hunger. In the daytime, during work, or on the way to and from work, I studied the banana groves, orange groves and mango trees. At night when it got really dark and everyone was asleep, I sneaked out, climbed the trees and stole fruit. Oranges were my favorite, because they were sweet. And each orange tree had a lot of fruit. I could pick one, and no one would know the difference.

Even though we knew that stealing would bring death, we still stole. One of my friends decided to steal a duck and some fish from the pond. He did not get caught. But then he got caught trying to steal a cow's tail from a living cow. He sneaked up beside the cow, petting her to make sure that she was calm. He carefully placed the cow's tail on the branch of a tree then with an axe tried to chop her tail off. Comrade Hai caught him in the act. To our surprise, Comrade Hai did not kill him on the spot. Instead he had his cook prepare a big meal for him. After the young man had finished eating, Comrade Hai let him lie down to rest on a mat. Just before the young man, with his belly full of food, fell asleep, Hai and his evil partners killed him by stomping on him with their tire sandals until he died. He screamed for mercy, but no one dared to help him.

The stories of their evil deeds spread among the villagers, and our fear of Hai intensified, like a fire grows when wood is added to it. I believe that they did those things to make the people afraid to revolt. The new villagers were controlled by fear, like elephants at the circus, who fear their master. There were only a few Anka and a lot of new villagers. We outnumbered them, but we feared them. No one dared to look into the eyes of Comrade Hai. I did get a glimpse of his face once. His eyes were big, red and scary. His face looked like that of a man under the influence of drugs.

CHAPTER 14

The "Hospital"

One evening after a very long day of work, I was extremely exhausted. I waited in line for my ration. After the cook gave me my portion, I took it home to eat, because the soup was watery; I wanted to add vegetables to it to make it more filling. There was neither salt nor meat in the soup. It had no nutritional value. Monsoon rains had made the path between the town commune and my house very slippery. I fell down and spilled my dinner on the muddy path. I tried as hard as I could to pick pieces from it out of the mud, but the rain mixed it with the muddy water, and I could not see it. I went home crying with frustration and feeling very hungry.

When I got home my father inquired about what happened. I told him. He said, "Heng, go back to the commune, tell the cooks what happened and see if they will give you another bowl."

"No, Pa!" I cried, "They will kill me if I ask for a second ration!"

Dad shouted at me. "You must go, Heng, or you will starve to death!"

"Then let me die!" I said angrily.

My father was thin and malnourished, but even with his skinny figure he still had pride. I was being disrespectful to him. He shouted back at me, "I am your father! You must obey me!"

"You can kill me, then, Pa, if you want, but I am <u>not</u> going back to the commune!" I answered defiantly.

"All right! I am going beat some sense into you if I have to!" I had made my father very upset. He yelled at me, "You stay here until I come back!" He grabbed a knife and walked out into the rain toward a bamboo bush. Soon he returned, soaking wet, with a whip in his hand. My mother tried to stop him from spanking me, but he refused to listen. He beat me several times with that stick. In great pain, I begged for mercy.

"I have learned my lesson, Pa!" I yelled at him. But he continued beating me until my mother came and put her body between his and mine. I could not get up. It did not take much to push my thin body to its limit. My mother came to pick me up. "See what happens, Son?" Mom said in a loving, but scolding way. "You have a strong will, Heng. You know that! But you must submit to your Pa. He is your father." Mom washed my bloody wounds with a wet rag and put me to bed.

In fairness I must say that my father was a good man. He had strong will, but he was a gentle and reasonable man, a man of few words. He had spanked me only two times before this. I knew he loved me even in the middle of our difficult times.

I became very sick after that day. I was bedridden for several days and could not go to work. My weak body needed nutrients and medicine. We had neither. I began to think that I would not recover. In the middle of the night my mother went to comrade Hai and requested food and medicine for me, but she returned empty-handed. She said to Dad, "You must take your son to the hospital at Som-Mo-Nous! We have no food or medicine for him here. He has a bad case of dysentery and can't walk. He is dying."

That night my father and brother carried me through the rain to a place called "Som-Mo-Nous." They tied each end of a hammock to a long bamboo stick, put me in it and set the sticks on their shoulders. My mother walked beside me, constantly calling out my name to make sure I was still alive. It was hard for them to walk on the wet and narrow dike. My father and brother were weak and fragile. They could hardly walk themselves. With the extra weight on their shoulders, they staggered. Several times they stumbled and fell to their knees, but they got back up and pressed on.

Rain poured down. Flashes of lightening split the black sky, giving brief glimpses of the path. Thunder echoed through the night. I was completely aware of everything. I felt as if it were my last night to live, and I tried to remember everything. The love of my family was overwhelming. Here they were, carrying me on their shoulders to get help, while they themselves were so weak. Physically they were too weak to do this, but their love for me gave them strength. "Come on son!" Father tried to encourage Cheang to keep moving. He stumbled and fell to his knees. But he got up again and went on.

Som-N-Mous was an old Buddhist temple, which Anka had converted to a "hospital". It was also known as "the undertaker's house", because no one who entered this place as a patient ever walked out. When we arrived there, they had no beds left inside, so the hospital keepers told my parents to leave me outside on a bed under the patio. Then they ordered them to leave to go back to the village. My mother refused to leave me. She told them, "You can kill me if you want to, but I am not going to leave my son to die here alone." Cheang and Dad did not stay.

I don't remember anything about the next twenty hours. Later my mother told me what happened that night. She said that after I was placed on the bed outside, I started to breathe heavily and then lost consciousness. I struggled to breathe, gasping for air. She yelled for help, but no one responded. She thought I was dying. Then with a sudden burst of energy I got up and started to the kick the wall and make loud noises. I got up on her knees, held the palms of my hands together above her head and bowed down to her and said, 'Oh, I honor you, Mother, full of grace. Please help me! Save my life! They took my soul and chained it under a big tree. If you want me to live, you must to give them sacrifices.' Mom was very frightened. The voice that spoke from my throat was not my voice. It sounded deep and loud like the sound of thunder. The voice said that the sacrifices must be made of hog's head, cooked whole chicken, steamed rice and incense sticks. Of course my mom could not get those things in such desperate times. By this time some of the young people who worked there came and stood around us to see what was happening. One of them had medicine and a spoon.

They tried to get me to open my mouth and take some medicine, but I refused. Another had an AK-47 with a bayonet attached to the end, ready to be used.

The one with the spoon said to my mom, 'There is no such thing as a demon spirit. Anka doesn't believe him. He is running a high fever, and he is hallucinating. We will give him medicine, and he will be better.' With the handle of the spoon, he tried again to open my mouth. My lips were cracked and split, and they bled, but my jaw was clamped shut. He tried several times with no success. Suddenly forceful and authoritative voice came out of my mouth; it said, 'If you don't believe us, we will kill all of you!' And with that the demon spirit left me. My body collapsed onto the bed.

Mom begged them, "Comrades, please, let me give him the sacrifice so we all can live. Please let me do it so my son can live." Mom was on her knees pleading with them.

They finally caved in and said, "Go and do whatever you need to, but do it secretly. Let no one know. We don't approve of it. Go now!"

Without hesitation Mom left in the dark to go back to the village. She stumbled and ran through the rice fields in the rain, afraid of the demon spirit. When she arrived home, she started to prepare the sacrifice. But there was no rice, no incense stick and no hog. She did not know what to do. The only person in town who had what she needed was comrade Hai. And he wouldn't believe her. Besides, she needed to keep it a secret; or I would be shot.

In desperation she went to the back yard, cut down a banana tree and chopped the trunk into five pieces. She took one piece of the banana trunk and pretended it was a hog's head. She took a second piece and chopped it into little bits and pretended that it was rice. The remaining pieces were split to make "incense sticks". Mom folded banana leaves to make seven small bowls and filled them with these items. After placing the pretend sacrificial objects beneath a tree, she raised her clasped hands and said, "Oh, gods, demons and spirits, listen to me! Here are the sacrifices for which you asked. I hope you are pleased with them and will give my son back to me."

Three days later mom came to see me. She was surprised and overjoyed when she saw me sitting up on my bed and eating rice porridge. I was alive! She couldn't believe it. "Son, the pretend atonement really works!" Mom was proud of herself for coming up with that idea.

She walked over to the comrades and asked permission to stay with me for a few days. Her request was denied. She stayed anyway, but received much harassment from these cruel Communists. They came to my bed and said, "Woman, go back to your village to work. You are not needed here. No work, no food." They kicked my mother and hit her head to make her leave. As much as I wanted her to stay, I begged her to leave. I was thinking that if I had been bigger and stronger, I would have beaten some respect into those young people. But I was weak and hungry and helpless.

Mom left that afternoon, but her love for me was strong. She returned after three days. I was so happy to see her walking through the temple gate. I called her, "Mom! Mom! Mom!" But she didn't recognize me. After she left my body had swollen to about three times its normal size. My thighs rubbed each other when I walked. Every part of my body was swollen. The young comrades told me to stay active. They said that if I stayed in bed and did not exercise, I would die. They said that if I wanted to live, I should eat whatever I could catch and get lots of exercise.

Mother wept when she recognized I was her son. She knew that many people swelled up before they died. But I reassured her that everything was okay. "I found favor with the comrades, Mom." She wiped a tear in disbelief. "Yes, Mom! They let me help them cook for the people here, and I get plenty of rice to eat."

"But how did you do that?" Mom was still puzzled.

"A few days ago I walked around to where they were cooking. The fire under the stove was dying out, and I brought wood for them. After that they told me to help them with the cooking."

Being a cook's helper during a time of starvation was a tremendous blessing and privilege. It made the difference between life and death. Once my mother knew that I was going to be all right, she left with a peaceful look on her face.

Each morning I got up early, regardless of the weather. I went for a swim in the pond behind the building. From the pond I collected snails, frogs, small fish, tadpoles, crabs and green plants. I cooked them and mixed them with my rice and ate them for proteins and vitamins. Since there were no spices such as salt and sugar added to my cooking, everything tasted bland. Salt and medicine were the most precious commodities in those days. Salt could be exchanged for an equivalent weight of gold or diamonds. A capsule of penicillin was worth a karat of diamonds or an ounce of gold. When people are dying, gold and diamonds are useless, but food and medicine become priceless. I wished that I had enough food for everyone there, but I scarcely had enough for myself. With better nutrients and sufficient food, my body began to heal. I became stronger, the swelling came down, and I began to put on some muscle.

Many sick people were carried into the temple, and so far none of them had recovered and left. People died there every day. They were buried in the orange grove behind the temple. Each grave there held ten to twenty bodies. The air smelled badly, and the orange trees died. When it rained, the graves flooded and corpses floated to the surface. After a while there was no ground left in which to bury dead bodies. So they began to cremate them. Whenever a new patient was carried to Som-Mo-Nous, I tried to see if any of them was my relative. I prayed to the gods that none of my relatives would ever come to this place. But of course I did not know to which gods I should pray.

What little religious training I had received had come from the Buddhist temple and my parents. I knew that there was a heaven and a hell. And as a boy I was taught that I had to do a lot of good deeds, like helping the poor, telling the truth, and giving money, to get to heaven. I knew that I was not going to heaven, and I was afraid. Sometimes at night, when I closed my eyes to go to sleep, I saw pictures of people with chains around their necks, bald and starving, shouting for help, with their hands raised in agony. Even after my bed was moved inside the temple, I was still afraid of dying. All the people who were dying were taken outside and left under the patio. When they died, the undertakers carried them away on a stretcher to be burned in the furnace.

Someone told me that my father's younger brother, Uncle Cheang, was here, too, in another building. I went over there to look for him, but I couldn't identify him, because everybody looked the same—like skeletons. In that building there were two rows of beds against opposite walls. I walked along the aisle, looking for Uncle Cheang. All the patients were either lying or sitting on their beds. The odor was overwhelming. I covered my nose. I heard a familiar voice calling out my name, "Heng!" I turned, and there was my uncle, dying in his bed. Once he had been strong, tall and good-looking. He had been a policeman who worked for the customs service in Cambodia, and had looked really handsome in his uniform, with his pistol at his hip. Now his body was wasted and shriveled, like a dried-up prune.

"Uncle Cheang?" I answered in disbelief.

"Heng, my nephew!" His voice was little more than a whisper. He was struggling to breathe and could not raise his head. I put my hand under his head and with my other hand began to help him get up. He said, "No! Leave me down." My heart broke, and I don't remember anything else. My uncle died that day, all alone, and his body was burned, along with five others.

After that, each day seemed long. So many people were dying, and there was nothing I could do to save them. I fed them with rice soup, but it did not help. I did not want to stay there anymore. So after three months I went to ask permission from the comrades to return to my family. I came in as a sick boy and left as a survivor. I had come to Som-Mo-Nous with black shorts and a shirt, and I left with the same shorts and shirt on. I had nothing else with me.

That night, before I left Som-Mo-Nous, I dreamed that my father and I went swimming in the lake. People were chasing us and shooting us. We swam with all our might. I got to the shore and waited for my dad but he was drowned. In my dream I cried out in grief, "Dad!" But he was gone.

CHAPTER 15

Father's Last Days

I was anxious to meet my family and to find out what had been happening there—especially to my Dad. I had lost him once before, and I didn't want to lose him again. Som-Mo-Nous was not on my mind at all. I was so happy to leave that place behind. I was amazed as I walked on dikes through the golden rice fields. They stretched for miles—all the way to the horizon. I felt as if I were the only person alive on earth. I still could not believe that I had walked out of Som-Mo-Nous alive. Out in the open fields, which stretched as far as the eye could see, golden stalks of grain swayed back and forth, stirred by the winds of December. Seeing so much rice being produced, I wondered why people were starving.

The cool morning had turned into a blazing hot afternoon by the time I made it into the village. I entered the same gate through which my father and mother had carried me on our way to Som-Mo-Nous months ago. My father was the first person to see me. When he saw me, he acted as if he had seen a ghost. He called out my name and started to cry. At first I didn't recognize him, but his strong, familiar voice verified that he was my father. He was so sick and weak and malnourished that he had to support himself with a stick. He walked carefully and slowly and looked as if he were a hundred years old, and he smelled badly due to the effects of dysentery and cholera.

"Father!" My heart broke as I embraced him. I could feel every bone, every rib in his body.

"Son! Heng! You are alive!" Father said in disbelief.

"Yes, Father, I am alive." No more words came from either of us for a long time as we stood in each other's embrace. I cannot recall ever being hugged before. Cambodian culture does not include much hugging. Not one time had I ever seen my parents hugging each other. Nor had I ever heard my mother or father say, "I love you" to each other. Affection was precious and rare. That is why I shall never forget this special moment that my dad and I had together that afternoon.

I helped him up the steps and into the Buddhist temple. Once it had been regarded as a holy place where people would take off their shoes and bow down before entering it. Now it had been turned into Anka's "Health Center." We had no shoes to take off. Without bowing, we entered the building. My father said to me, "I am really sick. I have had dysentery for several weeks now. I am going to ask Anka for a rabbit's pill." (Rabbit's pill was made of grass root, rice husk, a small amount of brown sugar. It had absolutely no medicinal affect, but father wanted it, because he could taste the trace of sugar in it.)

At the desk Dad opened his hand when the "nurse" came. She did not look as old as I was. She gave him a handful of the pills and then shooed us away like dogs. "That's all you are going to get!" she said.

I walked my dad to our place. Anka had moved my family to a new place after I was taken to Som-Mo-Nous. It was a small, thatched-roof hut a few yards from a blacksmith shop. (Father could do anything he set his mind to. He was a good blacksmith and could make knives, machetes, sickles and other implements. He had begun to work in the blacksmith shop after I was taken to Som-Mo-Nous.) In this small thatched house I would soon experience great hopelessness, fear and despair.

To my surprise every one of my brothers and my mother was at the hut when I arrived. They looked as skeletal as my father did. I was the only one who had any meat on his body. I was happy to see each one of them, but my happiness quickly became despair. Father's frail body collapsed, and he fell down.

Mom and my big brother Cheang and I carried Dad to where Mom had spread some banana leaves on the ground. Because Dad had to get out of bed frequently to relieve himself, it was better for him to stay on the ground. Mom tried to help him up, but he was too weak. "Say Guech, I need some sugar on my tongue," Father whispered as he struggled to breathe.

"Sugar?" Mom replied, with fear and desperation in her voice. "Where? And how, sweetheart?"

"Go, beg comrade Hai, please," Dad said. "I want a taste of sugar on my tongue before I die." Sugar was a precious thing. It was almost impossible to obtain. Anka controlled everything. A few months before, people could barter and exchange gold, diamonds or clothes for food and sugar. Now it was not available. Everyone was dying, but comrade Hai, his followers and his family were well fed. They controlled everything —food, freedom and even our lives. They told us when to wake up, when to eat and when to die. At night comrade Hai's followers acted as secret police agents, walking from house to house, snooping for information and listening in on conversations. Every night people were taken out of their houses with their hands tied behind their backs. Hai and his men killed people for stealing one red pepper. They seemed to have no soul in their body. They derived pleasure from killing.

Starvation killed most of the men, and executions took care of the rest. We lived in an area called "Section Four"—probably the worst place in Cambodia. Comrade Hai was the man most feared in Section Four. No one could look him in the eye and live to tell about it. Asking Mom to see comrade Hai was like giving her a death sentence. But there was no one else to ask.

My mother showed her love for my father by going to see Comrade Hai. Trembling with fear, she walked out of our little thatched-roof house and went to see him, knowing that this could be the last time she would see her husband and children. Clasped tightly in her hand was a little clay cup. She was only 32 years old, but looked as if she were seventy. Starvation and hard times had aged her. I admired her courage.

"Comrade Hai," Mom said, mustering all her courage and looking down toward the ground.

"Yes, Comrade Sokah," he replied in a soft voice.

"My husband is the blacksmith. He has helped Anka a lot. He has served Anka with all his heart. Without any hesitation he has used his skills for Anka and has worked very hard." Mom tried to use her best verbal skills.

"Everybody works hard to serve Anka!" He snapped. "And that's how it should be!"

"Comrade Hai, my husband is dying. He is weak and cannot walk. He has dysentery. A little sugar would help a lot—just a spoonful, comrade Hai." Mom got down on her knees and begged.

"No sugar!" he yelled at her. "Go home!"

"You can do whatever you want to me—kill me if you wish, but I am not going back to my husband, a man who so faithfully served you, Anka, without sugar. He is one of the unkown old villagers. He began in 1973 to help Anka fight the revolutionary war. Is this the way Anka treats one of his own?" Mother spoke with conviction. After all, my father had been one of them, though not by his own choice.

No one had ever spoken to Comrade Hai like that before and lived to tell about it. He would usually fly into a rage and eat parts of that person's body for lunch.

"All right! Give me your cup and I'll give you some sugar. But don't come back, Comrade Sokah," he said, beginning to grow calm again.

"Thank you, Comrade Hai. My husband also thanks you."

With the priceless material in her possession, she came home as fast as she could. She sat next to my father and cradled him in her arm. She carefully dipped her finger into the brown sugar and put some on his tongue. Father closed his eyes and savored the sweetness. "It tastes so good, Say Guech!" Father spoke softly. "A little more?" Mother took the spoon, scooped out some more and placed it on his tongue. "Thank you, Say Guech," said Father gratefully. Then he closed his eyes and went to sleep.

Some people believed that sugar helped with fatigue and dysentery. In father's case, it made him worse. That evening my father was carried on a stretcher to Som-Mo-Nous—that awful place which I had just left a few days earlier, the place where I wanted none of my family to go. I wanted to cry when the men took him on a stretcher, but I couldn't. My eyes produced no tears. My heart was numb. Rage, bitterness and thoughts of revenge filled my mind. Anka was responsible for all this pain and suffering! I tried to think of a way to kill Comrade Hai and his followers. But they were healthy, strong and armed with AK-47's.

I knew in my heart that my father would not return from Som-Mo-Nous. No one had ever walked out of that place alive—no one but myself. I kept all of those thoughts a secret. I didn't share them with my brothers and mother until years later. Seeing my father being carried away that night brought to my mind the dream I had had a few days before. I hoped desperately that it would not come true.

Three days later Mother returned from Som-Mo-Nous, alone. She looked worn out physically and emotionally. Father had died in her arms shortly after they arrived at Som-Mo-Nous. His body had been burned in the furnace, along with five others. Father's death brought much pain to our family, and to me in particular. I was led to believe that I was responsible for it. The Cambodian people had a strange belief.

I told my mother about what I had dreamed a few weeks earlier. Mom said, "If only you had died! Then your father would have lived. But you are living. So your father had to die."

"What do you mean, Mom?" I asked her.

"You were born on the same day as your father. And you both have the same zodiac sign. That is 'the snake'." (We believed that parents and children who have the same Zodiac sign are not compatible with each other. One will have a higher "spiritual chance", and he will live, while the other will die.) "You have a higher spiritual chance. You live. Your father died." I didn't want to believe my mother. However, she explained to me that my sister Ly Heang and she had the same Zodiac sign, and that was why my sister had to die. For a long time I carried this guilt with me, believing that I was the one to blame for my father's death.

CHAPTER 16

On Our Own

By the middle of 1976 few men were left alive in Section Four. The only men walking around were Comrade Hai and his followers. Soon after Father's death, Cheang, my big brother, was taken away to join the older youth group. My mother and baby brother Thong were taken away, too. My younger brother and I were left with the younger youth group again. I would have to scrounge for food. To survive, I looked for opportunities to steal anything I could get my hands on. I asked myself, *Why starvation when there is food everywhere?* Rice was growing on the farms, along with fruits such as coconuts, papayas, mangos, bananas and oranges. I sneaked out late at night to gather food, while the rest of the people were asleep. The guards slept in their hammocks as usual, with their AK-47's next to them.

I knew that if I were ever caught, I would be executed. But I was determined not to die from starvation. Every night my anger grew stronger against this "Anka", Hai. Many ideas came across my mind. I thought about starting a gang. When the gang had enough people in it, we could steal Anka's weapons and kill Comrade Hai and his pets. But everyone was weak and paralyzed with fear. That idea was quickly abandoned. The thought of running away to another section occurred to me many times, but Meng, my younger brothers and the rest of my family would be punished by death. The Communists thought of many ways to trap us.

This was the darkest time of our family's life. Shortly after our father's death, his parents and younger sister were taken to Som-Mo-Nous. They all died. My grandmother died from a centipede bite on her leg. Her body was too weak to fight off the infection. Grandpa and Aunt Keang died from starvation.

My brother Meng and I were taken into the jungle to clear the forest for more farmland. We did not know where the rest of our family was. We worked and slept out in the open field. At night it got cold. In the daytime it was hot. Anyone who complained about the living conditions would be killed by suffocation. The comrades would cover the offender's head with a plastic bag and leave him to die.

One of the happier days occurred when I heard that another group of Anka had come to take over Section Four. The Communist party had developed great mistrust among themselves. There were four main groups—the northern, western, eastern and southern. Once this new group arrived, they said that Comrade Hai and his followers had committed treason against Anka and must be punished by death.

They tied them all up and made them walk to a place called Watt Phnom, where interrogations and executions took place. Comrade Hai confessed that he had killed more than 70 innocent men. He had also raped a pregnant woman, killed her to keep h er from talking and buried her in the sand by the river. We never saw him again. People said they beat him so badly that every one of his bones was broken. He cried for mercy, but none was given.

My sinful soul found satisfaction in the news, but the new regime of Anka was no better than the previous. The workload remained the same. The "porridge" (rice soup) was still watery and had no nourishment or taste. However, they did allow us to get out of the village to look for food in the river and on the farms when we were not working.

With this new permission, I went to the river to collect mussels, took the meat out of their shells and preserved it with salt that I stole from the cafeteria. Then with green papaya I had stolen, I mixed it with the preserved mussels and made pickles.

More than a year passed before my younger brother Meng and I saw our mother and youngest brother. After the harvest season was over, the anniversary of the Communist Party came, on April 17, and we were allowed to visit our parents. I was told that Mom and our little brother Thong were at a place called Cke Koun (which means "Puppy"), far out in the bush. It took a whole day of walking to cover those 20 miles. But when Meng and I arrived at Cke Koun., no one was there. The group had moved to another place called Putrea. We tracked them down and found my mother and Thong living under a big tree in the open field.

We were very happy to see each other, but there were no hugs, and no words such as "I missed you," or, "I love you." I am not sure whether it was the culture or the numbness of our hearts that kept us from expressing our true feelings. Mom looked much better than she had the last time I had seen her. She had more flesh on her bones, but still she looked worn out. Her unique smile, with her front tooth framed with gold, was like a picture—priceless in such a time of despair. (Mom's front tooth had been capped with gold when she was 14 years old.) I brought her food, and together we had a family reunion. It would have been perfect if Cheang, my big brother had been with us.

That night I had a dream. I saw Cheang coming to meet us under that tree. He was healthy and strong. I got up really early that morning and told Mom about it. "Mom, in a dream last night I saw my big brother coming to see us. He told me that he needed a blanket." As soon as the sun rose, my dream came true. We saw a figure that looked like Cheang walking toward us. As the figure came closer and closer, we could see that it was Cheang.

As far as I remember, I have never had any other dreams come true like these two dreams. As Cheang walked toward us, I experienced a moment of spiritual curiosity. I began to question whether there was a God. But my curiosity quickly vanished when Cheang left the next day, and I was ordered to go to work.

CHAPTER 17

Rats and Snakes

Cambodia was infested with rats, especially during and after the harvest. Some wild rats grew almost as big as a cat. Instead of sending us back to the youth group, the man in charge of my mother's group allowed my younger brother and me to stay with them. Our job was to kill wild rats. He said I could eat the meat, but he wanted to have the tails brought to him at the evening. He wanted a count of how many rats we killed each day. Also he used them as evidence that I had been out there to work. "Rats eat rice," he said. "Anka needs you, Heng and Meng, to destroy them, or we will all go hungry again."

I was sure that this man was lying. We could let the rats eat all they wanted and still have enough rice to feed everyone in Cambodia. Later I found out that the Communists were shipping rice to China in exchange for weapons. But at the time I was happy to kill rats.

Early in the morning, while it was still cool, I left for the rice fields to look for rats. I carried a small shovel about two feet long, made of steel pipe, with a razor-sharp edge. Rats lived in holes that they dug into the dikes that formed the borders of the rice fields. Unfortunately, where rats live, snakes do also. Snakes ate the rats. And most snakes in Putrea were poisonous. King Cobras, Termite-hill Cobras, Water-buffalo Cobras and other poisonous snakes were there.

One morning, when I was out in a rice field, I saw a pile of rice stalks about the size of a Volkswagen Beetle. Rats normally would be found in such a pile. I poked the pile with my shovel. The rice pile moved! I stepped back a few paces and waited. Suddenly a huge snake stuck its head out toward me, flashing its forked tongue in and out. It tried to bite me. I stepped back and with great fear took off and ran away as fast as I could in a zig-zag pattern. I stumbled a few times and fell down in the ankle-deep water of the rice paddy. I could hear the sound of the snake chasing me. The rice stubs bent down as the snake moved. When I stopped, it stopped also. It appeared to be a King Cobra, eighteen or twenty feet long. I was too afraid to move, so I stood still, ready to strike the snake should he come close to me. He popped his head up to look when he was about 20 feet away. He moved his head back and forth. His head was about the size of my thigh. He was the biggest snake I had ever seen. He would make a lot of food. With one eye closed I took careful aim and threw the only weapon I had—my shovel—at him, as hard as I could. He ducked his head down and started to chase me again. I had blown it!

Now the only thing I could do to save my life was to run. I ran as far as I could, stopping occasionally to look back and catch my breath. My heart pounded like a big drum in my chest. I didn't want to die in the jaws of this beast.

After a while I could no longer hear the snake pursing me, so I stopped running. I thought it was safe. Then I began to wonder how I would kill it. *It would feed a lot of people,* I thought. *But how can I kill it? If only I had a hand grenade or could burn the field. But that would be too dangerous. The whole country might be consumed, and Anka would kill me.*

I needed to get my shovel back. I stood there for a while, trying to catch my breath and gather my thoughts. I decided to go back to search for my shovel. I retraced my steps. The muddy water revealed the path. The shovel stood in the rice field where I had thrown it. I grabbed it and ran for my life.

The sun shone straight down on the top of my head. It was noon already; and I had not yet killed a single rat. I must bring some rat's tails back to show the leader; or he would think I had been playing.

He would send my brother and me back to the youth group. I searched hard for rat holes along the dike; but just then I saw a fox running a few hundred feet away. *One fox gives more meat than a rat,* I thought. I decided to chase after him. At first he ran slowly, and it seemed I might be able to catch him. Once he stopped and stood there in the middle of field, looking at me. I tried to sneak closer to him. He started to run again—faster this time. I sprinted after him as if running a hundred-meter dash. He left me in the field, gasping for breath.

In another field not far away from there I dug into the ground, looking for rats. As I dug into one rat burrow, I would see a rat's tail sticking out. I grabbed the tail, intending to yank the animal out, swing it around and smack its head against the ground. Just as I grabbed the tail, the rat spun around and bit me on the top of my right index finger. It held on to my finger. I shook it until it fell to the ground. It tried to escape. Pain ran up in my finger. Blood dripped. I sucked the injured finger and spat the blood out. The wounds hurt, but I preferred being bitten by a rat over being bitten by a Cobra or some other snake!

The rat ran. I chased after it, with my shovel raised above my head, ready to strike should I catch up with the rat. It entered another burrow at the base of a wild prune tree. No rat was going to bite me and get away with it!

[Being out in the open field by myself, without Anka barking orders at me, kept me from becoming psychotic. This was the only time of my life under the Communist regime when I had any control over my life. In everything else Anka told me what to do. Chasing rats allowed me to vent my anger, frustration and fear. Those moments of freedom, when no one was there to oppress me, made me long to be set free. The rest of the time I felt like a bird in a cage.]

With my shovel I dug into the burrow at the base of the prune tree. Summer heat had hardened the ground. But my hands had developed thick calluses; they were like leather gloves. (My feet were even tougher than my hands. The calluses on my feet were so thick from walking without shoes that thorns or broken glass would not harm me if I accidentally stepped on them.)

The swishing sound of a rat confirmed that it was still in the burrow. It screeched. I continued to dig with my shovel, stopping occasionally to scoop the loose dirt out of the hole with my hands. Suddenly the little burrow lost its bottom and collapsed to a small cave a few feet in diameter. As the dust settled, a snake popped his head up only inches away from my face! I had never seen a live snake this close before. Shock and fear came to me at once. Cobra! Don't breathe, Heng, I told myself. Any movement might cause the cobra to strike. I held my breath. Finally I could hold it no longer. I could feel the pain in my chest from lack of oxygen. Grabbing a quick breath, I swung the shovel at the cobra. It ducked its head down, and I missed. I quickly ran a few feet away from it. I wondered why it had not struck me. This was not Cobra behavior. I knew beyond a doubt that it was a Cobra, the most deadly snake in Cambodia; it had the telltale "U" marking on the back of its hood.

The snake was still in the cave, coiled like a water hose. It was most dangerous in that position. How am I going to kill it? I wondered. I came up with an idea. With the sharp edge of my shovel, I cut a piece of tree branch about four feet long. Holding the stick firmly in my left hand, I picked up pieces of hard dirt from the ground and got ready to throw them at the snake, should he raise his head again. When the snake's head emerged from the hole, I started to throw dirt clods at him. The snake crawled out, with his tongue flashing through the air. I ran from side to side, trying to confuse him. Then I struck him with my stick. This broke his back. He crawled back into the den and coiled himself, preparing to strike if I should get close. I threw more dirt clods at him, trying to injure him even more. He crawled out of the hole to attack me, but with the stick I finished him off with a blow to the head. He twisted and shook for a little while and then remained still. Once I felt confident that he was dead, I cut his head off with the edge of the sharp shovel, put him on my shoulder and walked back to the camp. This would make a good lunch and possibly dinner for the family. I showed my catch to the man in charge. He told me that I was fortunate not to have been killed by this snake, and he agreed to accept the snake as a token of my day's labor.

Many people were killed by snakebites. A green snake bit a friend of mine on the cheek. Half of his face swelled up like a balloon, and then the flesh rotted away. Cobras are very poisonous. No one could survive a bite from this snake. No snakebite serum was available anywhere in the whole country. The snake's venom was so toxic that people would live only a few minutes after being bitten.

CHAPTER 18

Move to Section Three

My brother and I stayed with our mother at Cke Koun until the end of the summer of 1977. Just before the monsoon season arrived, Anka ordered us to go back to the village. At the village they told us to get ready to move again to a new place. When Anka told someone, "You will be sent to a new place," they usually meant "to a place of no return" (a place of execution.) Our family was very fearful, but we were ready. Each day we lived as if it were our last day to live. Each morning, when we awoke, we were thankful for one more day of life.

We had less food to eat in the village. There were no snakes or rats to kill. We had only the rice porridge, and it was not enough. Grubs, worms, caterpillars, crickets and grasshoppers were the extra proteins with which I supplemented my diet. Once I stole a piece of cowhide rope, and my brothers and I ate it, pretending that it was beef jerky.

Convoys of 10-wheel trucks came into town one night. Anka came to our house and told us to get into the back of a truck. We stood among many others, packed like sardines. Once the trucks were full, the convoy moved down the road toward some unknown destination. It had been a long time since I had ridden in a vehicle. It was quite different from walking. The convoys zoomed through the night. The moon was full, and the stars were bright. For a while I could see tall buildings along the highway, and then only trees and bush country.

The truck drove for a couple of hours before it slowed down, yielding to people working along the road. Along the highway, on both sides, thousands of people were digging. Each person had a shovel and a hoe in their hand. As the truck came closer, they stood up and looked at us. Meng, my younger brother, stood next to me. We were the last two people in the very back, while my mother and Thong were in the middle.

"Brother Cheang!" Meng shouted. "Brother Cheang! Mom! Brother Cheang!" Suddenly Meng jumped off the moving truck. I tried to stop him, but I was too late. Meng landed on his knees and his hands.

"Mom, Meng fell out of the truck! Tell the truck driver to stop," I yelled as loud as I could. Mom shouted at the driver, but he could not hear. He kept on driving.

In a panic, everyone in the back of the truck shouted to the driver to stop. "Stop the truck! Stop the truck! Someone has fallen out!" After a while he heard us and stopped. Mom and I jumped off the truck and ran to find Meng. By the time my I got there, the workers had picked him up and moved him off the road. His knees and the palms of his hands were all covered with blood, and he was crying.

"Brother Cheang!" he said, "I saw Brother Cheang, Mom!"

"Yes, Meng," I agreed, "I saw him, too. He was standing by the road a few hundred yards back." Mom and I picked Meng up and carried him back to the truck.

The truck driver interrupted us by saying, "Get back in the truck! We still have a long way to go!" I hoisted Meng up, and some people on the truck helped to lift him in. The people standing by the highway were ordered back to work, and the truck rolled on.

Meng was still crying. Mom and I checked him for signs of broken bones. He was okay. I told him that if he ever jumped like that again, I would beat him until all his bones broke! But I didn't blame him for doing that. The anxiety and the feeling of insecurity that came from being shipped to a graveyard made me want to jump out of the truck, too. I was scared. We all were scared. We all felt like sheep being taken to the slaughterhouse. And there was nothing we could do about it.

Meng and Mom and Thong wept silently together while I nursed my anger and bitterness toward those people who called themselves "comrades" and yet treated us worse than enemies. They were hypocrites and liars. They said that in the Communistic regime everyone would be equal and happy and that everything would be plentiful. The only plentiful thing was sorrow and starvation, the separation of families—and death. My anger was so strong that I vowed I would one day kill a Communist.

"Wake up, Heng! We are here," Mom said.

"Okay, Mom. Where are we?" I asked her.

"I don't know, Son, but we need to get our belongings together and get ready for our orders." We did not have many belongings. Each one had a small duffle bag of possessions. Anka said that only the rich imperialists had many possessions, and that these people must be destroyed. Therefore we had very few possessions: a bag of clothes, blanket, and cooking utensils. Mom still had an Omega wristwatch and two photographs—one of hers and Dad's wedding and a picture of our family. She hid them in the hem of her sarong (skirt).

"Get out!" the driver said. We all jumped out of the truck and waited along the highway for further directions. It was about six o'clock in the morning. Normally, this would be time for us to get up and go to work. Two men walked toward us. One appeared to be in his fifties, the other in his late thirties. They looked healthy and well fed. The older man walked with a slight limp. The younger looked big and stronger. We were relieved to see that they were not carrying AK-47's. And there were no gravesites to be seen. The older one appeared to be the leader. He was walking in front. They came over to the crowd. The older man cupped his hands around his mouth and spoke as if through a bullhorn, shouting his name and where we were. "Our comrades and Anka welcome you to Section Three of Cambodia. You are in O-nha village next to the Small and Big Mountain. We need you here to help us grow crops and rebuild our country!"

The despair and the fear of being executed turned to happiness, and a little seed of hope took root in my heart. Section Three was known to have more food, and we had heard that Anka was less aggressive; they didn't kill as many people here as in Section Four. And yet I was afraid to really believe any of this. I wanted to experience it first, before I believed it.

Comrade Seng made his announcement again. His words seemed like a ray of light, splitting the darkness. "Our comrades have prepared food for you. We expected your arrival. If you cross the road and follow me, I will take you to the cafeteria." He announced it again, " Food!" The sound of that word was like thunder echoing before rain in a drought. Our skeletal bodies needed nourishment badly. We stampeded to the cafeteria, and there, waiting for us on the table was a big plate of thick, hot rice porridge, with a spoon beside it. They even provided us with chili sauce. The soup was filled with meat and rice. It was the most food we had ever had in one meal in several months.

Our new house was built on stilts and had a thatched roof. Its bamboo floor was suspended about eight feet above the ground. The roof was leaky. We could see the sky. When it rained, we got soaked. The bamboo floor was old and also had several holes in it. The house was just one room, about 20 feet square. Mrs. Sim and her five children slept on one side. Mom and my brothers and I slept on the other side. Their feet touched ours when we slept at night. Mr. Sim had been taken away in the night by Anka about a year before. He had been killed because of his involvement with the previous government; he had been a captain in the army. Mrs. Sim had four daughters and a son named Rath. Actually the house was more than large enough for our two families, because we had so few possessions.

A few days after we arrived in Section Three, Mrs. Sim's older two daughters, who were 14 and 16 years old, escaped to the next village, where food was said to be more plentiful and working conditions were not as rough. Rath and his two sisters, my younger brother, Meng, and I were taken to join the youth force at the Buddhist temple. They gave us the same treatment as before—hard work and not enough food.

CHAPTER 19

Life in Section Three

Comrade Sok was our new leader. He was short and had a big mouth. He had a red birthmark on his Adam's apple. At five o'clock each morning he would kick the doors open, blow his whistle and shout, "Get up! It's time to go to work!"

If a person did not do as he said, he would kick them in the stomach. Most people were still fast asleep at that time in the morning. We all slept in a fetal position to keep ourselves warm, because we had no blankets. Fleas and ticks came through the cracks in the floor and feasted on us.

We marched out to work in the field as before, rain or shine, and worked twelve to fourteen hours a day. Sometimes we waded through neck-deep water to get to our workplace. Swimming through the field was not unusual during the monsoon.

During a meeting Comrade Sok said, "No one can escape from our youth place. Our comrade spies are downstairs guarding you. They are ordered to shoot any enemy of Anka. You may not go down to relieve yourself. Do your business from up here!"

Meng was only 10 years old then. He developed an anxiety about being separated from Mom. Several times he woke up in the middle of the night and sat up, kicking and sweating profusely and screaming, "Big, big! He is so big! Help! Help me, Mother!"

"What is so big, Meng?" I demanded. But he never communicated during these times. He would cry and scream for half an hour, then collapse and fall asleep. When I asked him about what had happened the night before, he would not know what I was talking about.

After several such episodes Comrade Sok became very impatient with us. Even though his place was private and outside of our compound, he would show up and demand that Meng and I calm down or, as he said, "The consequences will be severe!" I asked him to allow Meng to go back to the village to visit Mother. He refused. As the big brother, I had to do something. We decided to sneak out.

"Wake up, Meng," I whispered softly and carefully to Meng's ear while patting his head. We are going to see Mom. He quickly awakened when he heard me say, "Mom." He held my hand as tight as he could. We both were scared. "Follow me, and keep quiet," I instructed him. "If anything happens to me, just run. Okay?"

We both climbed out of the window and down one of the wooden posts that supported the floor. The comrade's spies were fast asleep in their hammocks, which were suspended between the posts, one of which we were climbing down. Their AK-47's, equipped with bayonets, were leaning against the posts next to them.

"God, please help me," I whispered within my heart. I was tempted to grab one of the guns, but because I did not know what I would do with it afterward, I decided against stealing it. Had I known how to shoot a gun, I may very well have killed every Communist sleeping there that night. In the darkness we ran through the bush and out into the open rice field. We swam across the creek. As we ran along the dikes, we slipped and fell several times. Meng kept a tight grip on my hand. Every little sound attracted our attention—the crickets, the wind against the dead brush, the howling of the coyotes. The fear of ghosts and the fear of stepping on poisonous snakes was constantly with us. But what we feared most was being caught by the Communists.

Yet the thought of seeing our mother gave us comfort and courage to move on. We made it to the highway. We looked both ways. Seeing no one, we crossed it. Our house was right in front of us. Since this was the monsoon season, floods had come, and the area in which our house was built, once dry land, was now full of water.

The house was suspended on stilts above the water. We swam to it, climbed the few front steps not covered by water, opened the door and crawled in next to our mother. Mom woke up. When she realized who we were, she was overcome with joy, and wept. There is no place like home. We slept with great comfort next to our mother, knowing that everything would be all right for now. We all savored those precious moments together.

Mom got up early in the morning and left for work. The three of us kids remained asleep. When I woke up, I felt something wet against my neck and on the mattress. I looked and saw blood everywhere on the mattress. Then I felt some stinging pain on my neck. I pressed with my finger around the pain and felt two little bumps on my neck. The first thought that came into my mind was that a vampire had sucked my blood. Blood was everywhere on my hands and neck. Then a feeling of relief overcame me when I saw a big, fat leech the size of a large cucumber next to me. Evidently the leech had attached himself to my neck while I was swimming the night before. I looked everywhere else on my body to see if there were any more leeches, but found none. Because the leech had injected me with anti-coagulants, I bled for several hours.

That afternoon, after I had carefully studied the area around the house and had found no one watching, I took the leech and placed it on a railroad track, which was located only a few hundred yards behind the house. I hid in the bush, waited until the train came and watched with delight as the train's steel wheels destroyed that offensive creature!

Mom returned from her work late at night. She brought us her portion of food to eat. I refused to eat it, because the food was not sufficient even for her.

"A spy has been in our house," Mom said. She added, "A few weeks ago they went through our bags and found a watch and a couple of photographs. Comrade Pai requested the watch, but I told him that without the watch, I couldn't tell time. He then said, "Do you want to know time it is, or do you want to live?" He then took it and said, "Anka needs to borrow this watch. Anka needs it more than Comrade Sokha."

Mom warned us not to talk at night, but to carefully listen for a spy's footsteps. They even waded through the water to come to our house so that they could eavesdrop on our conversations. But we stopped talking when they came.

Mom sewed two huge pockets on the inside of Meng's shirt and mine. The pockets were a handy place in which to hide things. Meng and I stayed with mother only a few days, and then we returned to the young people's compound. We went back the same way we had left—stealthily, in the middle of the night. Climbing up the posts to enter the building proved more difficult than climbing down. But we were determined, and we made it. The guards were sleeping, as usual, in their hammocks. Again I was tempted to get the gun and take revenge. Carefully and quietly, like burglars, Meng and I sneaked back into the building. With our clothes wet from swimming, we lay down and pretended to be asleep. My heart was ready to leap out of my chest because of the fear that Comrade Sok might have found out about our secret. But Meng stopped getting up in the middle of the night and screaming as he once had.

Because the compound contained many thousands of people, my few days of absence were not noticed. At least that's what Comrade Sok made us believe. Several times each month Meng and I sneaked out. Once Mrs. Sim asked if I could help Rath, her son, to sneak out also, because she was really missing him. On the next "sneak-out", the three of us went home together to see our mothers.

Anka knew everything. They knew when and how we sneaked out, and when we came back. I am not sure why consequences were not given to us. Maybe Meng's nightmares encouraged them to close their eyes. Maybe they thought it would be better for Meng not to be there at the compound, disturbing everyone.

Mom became very ill and was sent to the hospital at the foothills of "The Small Mountain." Being in Section Three instead of Section Four, her chances for recuperation were somewhat better. They had better care, food and facilities than Som-Mo-Nous. Small Mountain was much farther away than our previous house, and it was under a different authority. A permission paper was required to pass from one village to the next. If anyone was caught trespassing, they could be imprisoned without food or executed.

To our surprise, Comrade Sok gave us the pass to see our mother. Meng and I walked westward along the railroad. We jumped from one railroad tie to the next. Along the railroad were rice fields, green and healthy. The hospital was located a few blocks away from the railroad. Mom was not as sick as I thought she would be. She and my baby brother were malnourished, but not so seriously as a year or so before. She had the severe headaches and fever that signaled malaria. She liked it at the hospital, because she did not have to be out in the field.

To my surprise, I saw one of my father's younger sisters at the hospital. We spent a few hours visiting. "Every one of our family is dead, you know," Aunt Muy mourned, "My father, my mother, your father, my brothers and my sister are all dead. They all died because of sickness and lack of food, except Grandma. She died from a centipede bite on her leg. It became infected. There are only two left in my family: your Uncle Hor and I. And I am not sure about Uncle Hor. He may be dead, too." Aunt Muy tried to get me caught up with what was happening in our family's life. I already knew about it, but I listened to her venting any way. The news was never good. Each time I heard it, it opened old wounds, and my heart ached. *"I am going to kill a Communist,"* was the vengeful thought in my heart. Aunt Muy cried when she told me the stories. I couldn't. I had seen too much suffering and pain. And to cry was a sign of weakness for a man.

When it was time to leave, Aunt Muy said, "Wait. I've got something for you." She went outside the building and told me to follow her. She handed me a fishing rod made of bamboo sticks and said, "I want you to have it. Your aunt can't use it. I don't know how." She also gave me about 15 feet of 20-pound nylon fishing line and a good-sized fishing hook. This was perfect for fly-fishing. Fishing lines and hooks were rare at that time. Hardly anyone had them. They simply weren't available. This was a priceless gift. I thanked Aunt Muy and left her place, then went to say good-bye to my mother. "Heng, eat this before you go," Mom said. She gave me half of a boiled egg.

My eyes opened wide with surprise. "Where did you get this?"

"Your brother, Meng, brought it. He stole the chicken eggs from Anka's hen," she said with a mixture of pride and embarrassment.

"There is nothing wrong with stealing, Mom. You have earned it. They haven't paid you, " I said in a voice tinged with anger against the comrades.

"Meng," she warned, "you have to be careful. If they catch you, they will cut all your fingers off one at a time, and then they will cut your throat."

I also tried to scare Meng so that he would not do that again. "Stealing Anka's personal things is a serious crime—serious enough to bring death," I told him.

Chicken eggs were not supposed to be eaten. They were to be left to hatch. But Anka ate them, and so did we. Meng raided the chicken nest during daylight, placed the eggs into his pocket and ran to the railroad track. There he carefully hid them in a banana bush. He put stones into his pocket and pretended nothing had happened. The Communist spies chased him and caught him and demanded that he hand the eggs over to them. Meng pulled the stones from his pocket, handed them to the spies and said, "You wrongfully accused me. Where is your evidence?"

"We saw you with our naked eyes in the chicken house," they insisted.

"I didn't steal anything," Meng replied.

They left him alone then. Late that evening, while no one was looking, Meng went back to the banana bush and retrieved his prize. He boiled the eggs in the kettle. That was how we got boiled eggs that evening.

Meng refused to leave Mom and go with me, so I went back to the youth group alone. On the way back I stopped occasionally to do fly-fishing and caught several fish. I used frogs and flowers as bait. I cleaned the fish, preserved them carefully with salt and later sent them secretly to my mother.

Meng finally rejoined me with the youth group. I sent him back with preserved fish wrapped around his body, beneath his over-sized shirt. The food never made it to mom or my aunt. Anka searched Meng on his way and the food was confiscated. But they let him go to see Mom, because he had a permission slip from Comrade Sok.

Every time he went to visit Mom, he did not want to return. One time the Communists had to peel him off from Mom while he screamed at the top of his lungs, "No! I want to be with my mother."

Mom, of course, tried to gain favor with the Communists by encouraging Meng to go. "Go ahead, Son," she said. "Our comrades will be good to you." But Meng knew better. They were our enemies. They tied his hands behind his back like a criminal, put him on the back of their bicycle and took him back to the compound. They placed him in a room on the second floor, closed all the windows and locked the door behind them, intending to let him die there, but Meng escaped that night and ran back to stay with Mom.

Each day we struggled to survive. Starvation was a normal way of life; to be hopeless, illiterate, and decaying away seemed to be our fate. Our lives were in total darkness; for us there was no "light at the end of the tunnel". We had no contact with the outside world. We were nothing more than slaves, existing only to do Anka's work. Silence was the code of life. We dared not speak; being deaf and mute was a must. Our eyes photographed the horror like a film of bad memories. Each frame depicted only horrors, and nothing could erase them. Each morning, when I woke up, I wished it were a dream. But when Comrade Sok walked in with his loud whistle, I knew I was not dreaming. My goal each day was to make sure that I was still alive at the end of the day. I kept on thinking that maybe someone would come and rescue us from our misery.

Each day seemed long, each year like eternity. We struggled through the torment of the day, knowing that the coming night could be the night on which the death angel would come to visit us. Sometimes the thought of dying was actually a comfort to my weary soul. We have a saying in Cambodia: "Old people have death to lean upon; a child has his crying." I was not yet old, but the idea of dying was sometimes appealing. I could cry, but no one was there to help. Mom got well enough to be dismissed from the hospital and came back to the village. Meng returned to be with me. It didn't take him long to start missing Mom miserably again. So we began to sneak out again, in the middle of the night.

CHAPTER 20

Harvest Time

The rice field began to dry out, and the creek became narrower; the flood season was almost gone. The cold December wind was unpleasant to my skin, but bearable. All I wanted was to meet the basic needs of my family—to give them food, water, warm clothes and a place to sleep. I just wanted to see my mother, and to make that journey safely. Rath came with us whenever I let him.

[In America, the time between Thanksgiving and Christmas is the busiest of the year. People shop and sing and watch football and eat turkey, ham, sausages, apples and pecan and pumpkin pies. Many leftovers are thrown onto the trash can. At this time in my life, if I could have had the trash from America, I could have had a feast. But since I didn't know anything but hardship, and lived in such a dark world of oppression, I knew nothing of America. So jealousy never overcame me.]

The rice was almost ready for harvest by early December. The grain turned light green and golden. At this time our work was not as heavy. Our job was to be a scarecrow, chasing sparrows away to keep them from eating the grain. But Anka did not know that the scarecrow probably ate more grain than the sparrows! All of us picked grains from the stalks and at them raw. We chewed and sucked on the sweet-tasting grain and spit out the chaff. But when the spies came near, we swallowed the chaff also. Rice chaff is very abrasive, almost like broken glass. I was afraid it might cut my stomach or intestines. Often I wondered if I would die from it.

Toward evening, when it was time to come home, I grabbed a couple handfuls of grain, put them in my two pockets and took them to my mother. We waited until we had accumulated enough to cook a meal for the whole family. My younger brother, Thong, loved fresh cooked rice. We all loved it, but he seemed more excited about it than anyone else. Thong was almost five years old by early 1978. He was very malnourished. His belly was distended because of worms, and yet his chest looked like a skeleton—more so than ours. He was always quiet; he never cried, never complained. Maybe he was thinking that starvation and deprivation were normal. A little pot of rice brought so much happiness to our family. We took turns eating. While one person ate, the rest of us watched for Anka's spies. Sometimes we took turns with Mrs. Sim's family. We watched for them, and they watched for us.

We all determined to live, even by way of stealing. We knew stealing was wrong; but we believed that we were just taking what rightly belonged to us. My fly-fishing rod became very useful. I also became very skillful at catching fish in the water with my hands and feet. Sometimes I even caught snakes. We pressed our hands against the bottom of the pond and felt for fish. If the water was too deep, we used our feet. Once we felt a fish, we grabbed it. We had no container in which to keep the fish we caught, so we used our mouths, holding the fish between our teeth.

Some people died from the snakebites they got while fishing like that. Others died because of the fish they held in their mouths. In its struggle to get away, a fish would work its way into their throat and block their airway. They would struggle to pull the fish out by its tail, but that never worked; the fish got scared and thrust itself deeper into their throat. I made sure a fish was dead before I held it between my teeth!

Placing sickles into our hands, Comrade Sok and his comrades led us to the fields every morning to reap rice. Once we got to the field, we lined up facing the field and began to cut rice stalks with our sickles. We made bundles of stalks, tying each one with a string made of rice stalks. The bundles were left to dry in the field for a few days, and then another group would come with an ox-cart to take them back to the village for threshing. We harvested in the same way people did in ancient times. Once threshed, the grain was spread out on an asphalt street to dry some more. (No vehicles were allowed on the street in this season.)

After the grain was dry, it was separated from the chaff. There were two ways to do this. One way was to scoop up the grain and pour it slowly in the wind. The chaff would blow away, while the grain remained. The other way required more work. We placed the grain in a large bamboo tray and shook it. The grain remained on the bottom, while the chaff came to the top.

Once separated from the chaff, the rice was again spread on the street for further drying. Then it was taken to the mill, which was about a mile away. Young people were not allowed to go near the mill. That was an off-limits area. Another area that was off limits was a whitewashed building located between our village and the next one. Many people believed that the Chinese were there, doing some sort of experimental project. They also believed that this was a place where people were taken to be tortured and interrogated. Others told me it was a place for scientists to study agriculture. I was curious about it. The mystery was soon revealed.

In the fields I tried to work harder than the average person. I almost always did more than what was required of me. I did that for one reason—to stay alive. Every day Anka came by to check our work and our hands and faces. If people's hands were not dirty enough, and evidence of work inadequate, Anka took them away and killed them. So I kept my face and hands dirty all the time. I did this also because of my skin color, which is lighter than that of the average Cambodian. Had they found out that I was half Chinese, they would have would killed me. I always took a muddy bath before going to bed. I stayed dirty all the time. They never saw the true color of my skin.

One day I was on my way to work, as usual, walking in a line with other workers. The grain on the street caught my eyes. Quickly I looked around for Anka. Thinking that no one was looking, I sat down and rolled into the bushes. When it appeared that no one was pursuing, I crawled on my knees and elbows, like a lizard, to the grain on the street. I looked carefully left and right, then scooped up some grain and put it into my pockets. I had looked left and right, but not straight ahead. Suddenly, right in front of me, I saw an old woman. She stood with her legs spread apart and a big broomstick in her hand. She began beating me and yelling, "Thief! Dirty thief! Someone help me!" She was one of the "old villagers". Her heart was cold; she had no compassion.

I panicked. Not knowing what to do, I did the most natural thing—I got up and started running, only to be surrounded by Communist soldiers. They didn't waste any time on me. The soldiers were much older than I, and they had guns with them.

"You are an enemy Anka!" yelled one of them as he threw me to the ground. The grain fell out of my pockets, giving evidence against me. They were merciless. One man jerked both of my hands back behind my back and tied my elbows together with a rope. The ropes were tight; they made my flesh feel as if it were burning.

I'm dead, I thought. One of the men, who appeared to be the leader, picked me up by one elbow and planted me on my feet. "Anka will kill you!" he yelled. "You have committed horrible crimes—stealing and avoiding work!" They all looked alike in black pajama uniforms. Their faces looked mean.

"I am sorry, Comrade! Please forgive me," I pleaded. "I have worked faithfully for Anka for the last three years, rain or shine. I was hungry." I begged them with tears as they led me toward that whitewashed building. "I am sorry Comrade," I said again and again, pleading with the young man who was walking beside me. He did not respond.

They seemed to enjoy their work. After pleading did not work, I stopped crying and begging and walked with them in silence, accepting my fate. I was sure I was about to die. I did not want to go to the white building, but I had no choice. These people were sadistic. They kicked me, and when I lost my balance and fell down, they jerked the rope and pulled me back up. The tightness of the rope caused my arms to get numb. I could not feel my arms below my elbows. They led me on toward the whitewashed building.

We reached the gate that led to the building. There I saw people walking about, wearing white lab coats. Some were riding three-wheeled scooters. They looked like Korean or Chinese scientists. They had light skin and almond-shaped eyes. They spoke a language I had never heard before. But I didn't care who they were; I just wanted to live. Instead of taking me through the gate, the soldiers led me in the opposite direction— across the street to their compound. This was their village headquarters.

"Don't kill him yet," said the leader. "Let him work for three days and nights to make up for his crimes. Then kill him!" He walked into the building. The other soldiers followed him and left me there, standing outside in pain. I thought about escaping, but I was too afraid to try. I could not outrun them with my arms tied. I realized then how much fear my father must have felt when the Khmer Rouge took him into the jungle. So I had become like my father—a prisoner of the Communists, who refuse to believe there is a god. I was so lonely and scared and hopeless. I wished that I knew a supernatural being who could come to rescue me. I meditated on a prayer that I had learned at the Buddhist temple when I was younger. I didn't understand what it meant:

> Yang Ken Ke Ya Kam Mang
> Kach Ta Pang Ve Ra Ma Ne'
> Sa Ra Nang, Katcha Meg.

I repeated this again and again. I asked for the grace of my mother to rescue me. Many of us believed that the grace of our parents could help us in time of trouble. I asked for the spirit of my father to help.

A spy interrupted me: "You see that bucket? You carry the waste out and put it over there!" He took a sharp knife and cut the rope that held my arms. He looked worse than any of the snakes I had killed.

"Yes, comrade," I replied as I tried to shake feeling back to my arms. He walked back into the building to join his gang.

"How are we going to kill him?" I heard them talking .

"By electrocution!" exclaimed one voice.

"Yes! We will do that!" They all agreed.

I was terrified. All day I thought about how painful it would be to be shocked by electricity. Through the rest of that day and late into the night I carried buckets of human waste on my back, moving it from one area to another. For the first several hours they watched every move I made.

Later that night, while they were talking and not paying attention, I knelt down and crawled into the rice field. Soon I encountered a creek and crawled into it. I submerged my whole body under the water, exposing only my nose for air, and swam as quietly as I could to get away. Once I had gone far enough to feel safe, I stopped and looked to see if anyone was following me. Seeing no one, I climbed out of the creek and ran faster than I had ever run before.

As soon as I got close to where I had been living, I took my clothes off and waded into the river to wash the smell of human waste out of my clothes and off my body. Checking my body for leaches, and finding none, I took my customary mud bath and put my clothes on. I began walking slowly toward my mother's place. But then I realized that if they found me there, my mother would be killed as well. Not knowing where else to go, I returned to the youth compound. I thought that since there were many young people there, they would not be able to recognize me. All of us looked alike—bony and malnourished.

CHAPTER 21

The Vietnamese Invasion

The next morning I went to work as usual, except with more fear than ever before. I watched carefully for any Communist soldiers who might be walking toward me. I had a plan—I would run. Living in fear was miserable; it made the day seem much longer. They did not come after me that day. Nevertheless, I was still a fugitive, and I had no place to which I might run. They could come to get me at any time.

Later I found out why they did not come after me. The Communists had planned to kill everybody in the village. Many villagers said that the Communists were planning to call for a town meeting. Once everybody got inside the big building, they would lock the door; then set off a bomb and burn the building to the ground. I believe that this was the reason they did not come after me. They had "bigger fish to fry."

But their plan changed. Something happened that day that kept them from carrying out their murderous plan; the Vietnamese invaded Cambodia. Immediately all of the Communist soldiers in town busied themselves with moving out of town. They gathered all their people, placed their children and most of their possessions on ox-carts and quietly left town that night. At the time none of us knew why they were leaving. We did hear thunder echoing from far away. It was abnormal to hear thunder in December, but we suspected nothing else.

The next day I went to work as usual, but sent Meng home to be with our mother. With the sharp sickle in my right hand I cut and bundled rice stalks, while listening carefully to the thundering noise, which seemed to be coming closer and getting louder. Big Mountain was less than ten miles away from us, and the thundering noise was coming from that direction. The sound seemed familiar, much like what I had heard during the war. It sounded like artillery shells exploding. Comrade Sok also appeared to be disturbed by the noise, but he did not allow it to interfere with his ego. He went right on bossing us around with our work. "Come on, get on to work!" he shouted at us. "Don't pay attention to that noise! It's thunder!" He tried to lie to us.

People have come to rescue us, I thought. *I am going to be free!* Comrade Sok didn't go with the rest of the Communist soldiers. He remained with a few of his comrades to be our taskmaster. They carried no guns. "Work!" they commanded. We finished the day and went back to our compound. That night the Communists packed their belongings and left town in a hurry. Comrade Sok was too stubborn to leave. I wondered if perhaps he was addicted to his power and could not give it up. He remained to be our taskmaster for another day.

The next day he woke us as usual to go to work. We did as we were told; we marched to the fields. But we sensed that our world was about to turn upside down. We could have defied his order; but we were still too frightened. We could have killed him that day, because he was alone. His comrades had run for their lives.

I knew something really big was going to happen that day, and I wanted to be with my family. Once we were out in the field, I placed the sharp, serrated edge of my sickle against my left index finger then pulled the sickle against it quickly, with my teeth clenched and my eyes closed. Blood rushed out. I squeezed the cut to expel more blood and carefully dripped the blood into my right hand. With the blood I smeared my left hand, wrist and shirt, making it look like it was a major accident. I was in pain. The people working next to me saw the blood and yelled, "Accident! Comrade Sok, we have an accident!"

My plan worked. Comrade Sok came and checked my hand. Despite all of his Communist bravado, he was afraid of blood. That is why he had people killed by means of a plastic bag; it made no bloody mess. With a disgusted look on his face, he said, "Go to the center and get some medical help." He walked away. And so did I. That was the last time I saw his face. Many times I have wondered what happened to him.

I didn't go to the youth center. Instead, I ran home. There I met my mother and two younger brothers. We packed our few belongings got ready to go. We didn't know where to go, but we were ready. We sat there in the house, impatiently waiting for our freedom to be delivered.

Late that evening, Mrs. Sims' two young daughters and Rath came to join her. The two older daughters had not yet come. Mrs. Sims was anxiously waiting for them. She paced back and forth murmuring, "Where are they? Why don't they come?" My family was together, except that we did not know where my oldest brother was. We planned to search for him after the war. The thunderous sounds grew louder and louder. We stayed in the house and waited for the night. Mrs. Sim's two older daughters had still not made it home.

Early in the next morning people in the village scattered in every direction when army tanks, trucks and thousands soldiers on foot stormed into town. Meng and I carried bags, while Mom held the baby. Mrs. Sims was in a panic. Her two older daughters had not come, and she could no longer wait for them. She paced back and forth like a hen protecting her young in the presence of a hawk.

"Sokha,' Mrs Sim said to my mother, please keep my three children with you. I am going to the other village to look for my other two girls."

"Don't go! Stay, Mrs. Sim!" Mom tried to stop her, but could not. She begged Mom to care for her children, gave some instructions to the children and than ran off down the street. It was there that I observed again the love of a mother for her children. Even though she knew that her life was in danger, she went anyway to look for her daughters. This was unconditional love!

At this time I also learned another valuable lesson: Never make hasty decisions in a panic situation. Be patient. Let the dust of chaos settle down. Evaluate the facts, and then make an educated and deliberate decision. Mrs. Sim taught me this lesson—with her life. We were caught inside the battle zone. The Khmer Rouge soldiers were on one side of the village; the Vietnamese troops were on the other. Shots were fired, and bullets flew everywhere. People were screaming. Tanks kept on rolling forward, shielding the soldiers who walked behind them.

"Di!" The Vietnamese shouted. ("Di" means "Go" in the Vietnamese language.) We lay down on the ground next to the road, looking on with much fear for Mrs. Sim. She was trapped on the street. People were shooting at her from both sides. She ran a few steps back and then ran the other way. Both sides probably thought that she was their enemy. She was panic-stricken. I cannot forget that day. Right in front of my eyes Mrs. Sim was shot from behind by a grenade launcher. We called this projectile a "79"; it was an American-made weapon, shot from an M-16. Her body was blown completely off the street. Her children screamed and yelled, "Mother!" But we held them down. They cried, and we cried with them.

The battle in our village took only a few minutes, but the memories and the scars have lasted a lifetime. Once the shooting had died down somewhat, and I had begun to come down from the adrenaline rush, I realized that I was lying on the top of a fire ant nest, and those ants were having me for dinner! They bit me on every part of my body. I was in pain, but I did not dare to move. The Vietnamese chased the Khmer Rouges out of the village. Once the shooting was over, I ran and submerged myself in a pond in front of the house. Big, swelling red spots with tops like bubbles were all over my body. From the pond I watched Mrs. Sims' children as they ran onto the road to check on their mother.

We all tried to comfort them. The Vietnamese soldiers ordered us to return to our home. The town became quiet, like the calm after a storm. When we felt safe to get out of the house, I went with Mrs. Sim's children to see her body.

The bullet had hit her right buttock and destroyed it. She lay face down, in a thicket of thorns. That made her more decent. No one would recognize her. We left her there. Many times I have tried to erase that image of her from my mind, but it remains. The two older sisters came a few days later and took all three teenagers with them.

CHAPTER 22

Life without Law

With the Communists gone, there was no authority in sight. Free! We were as free as an eagle in the sky. The whole village and everything in it were at our disposal. It was like going to a buffet restaurant, with lots of food prepared and no chef in sight. Liberty had finally come. The darkness of the night was removed, and a new dawn began in our lives. The Khmer Rouge Communists had been chased like rats—out of town and into the forest.

"When the cat is gone, the mice dance." We were hungry, so I said to Mom, "Meng and I are going to get us some food." I also suggested that she should stay at home with the baby brother. I took Meng to the rice mill in town. Yesterday it had been off limits. Now no one was guarding it. In front of the building was a big mountain of golden grain—the fruit of our years of labor. Twenty feet to the left of it was a pond. Its water was stained with purplish blood, and several swollen bodies were floating in it. Bloodstains covered the ground around it. Flies hovered over it all like a swarm of bees. The odor was strong. I could see human bones and skulls lying beneath the shallow water.

The doors of the rice mill building had been left wide open. Meng and I were the first people there. Filled with greed, I told Meng, "Get some bags." We filled our bags half full of rice and tied them with strings. My bag weighed about 50 pounds, Meng's about half that. I could not believe that there was so much rice stored in the village while people were going hungry. Then it became clear to me that the Communists had purposely starved us. They wanted us to be weak so that we would not have the strength to rebel. They had muzzled the mouth of the working oxen. There was enough rice in that warehouse to feed the whole village for several years. After helping Meng hoist his load onto his shoulders, I sat down and raised my own load onto my shoulder. And we both staggered home.

All day we carried rice home, making forty or fifty trips. After we were too tired to carry any more, we dragged the bags down the street. Our house was full of rice bags upstairs and downstairs. We had enough rice to keep us from going hungry for a long, long time. People joined us, taking pleasure in stocking their homes with food. Once we had enough rice, I went to the cafeteria to get cooking utensils and salt. Then I went to the duck farm.

The ducks at the duck farm had been raised especially for the Korean scientists who occupied the white building, and for Anka's people. The farm, which was dominated by a large pond, was located behind the white building. There must have been thousands of ducks swimming in the pond. I grabbed some strings, gave some to Meng and told him to follow me. We chased and caught many ducks and tied their legs together with the strings. Meng and I counted them. We had caught fifty ducks! We butchered ten that day but kept the others alive for a future meat supply. What a feast! We hadn't had such a meal for more than three years. We ate and ate.

I was curious about the white building, so I pushed the gate open. No one was there yet. I went inside the center of the big building. It appeared to be a storage place. A three-wheeled car was parked in the courtyard, and the key was in it. I turned the key to start it, but the gas tank was empty. I pushed it into the building.

Inside I saw all kinds of bags and clay jars, and a wooden wheelbarrow. Some bags held fertilizer. On some bags I could not read the label, because it was written in a foreign language. Deep inside a closet I found several four-gallon clay jars full of brown sugar and honey. Anger and bitterness and sadness flooded into my heart all at once. I remembered my dad's last request before he died. In anger I picked up one of the jars and dashed it against the concrete floor to destroy it. Something brown came out of the broken jar. I stuck my finger into the substance and placed it on my tongue. It was honey.

I selected one jar and carefully placed it on the front seat of the car. Then I left the car and ran into the next room. There I saw all kinds of beakers, test tube, flasks, centrifuges, and glass case filled with colorful liquid chemicals. I could not read the labels on the bottles. But I figured that this place must be an experimental laboratory. I picked up one bottle and tried to read the label. It had a warning on it—a picture of a skull and crossbones. I figured that it was DDT, a poisonous chemical. I brought a few of the big cans to the car. I still had the whole building to myself. The old saying was proving true: "The early bird catches the worms."

I was almost finished with my tour of the white building when the rest of the villagers came in. They found the floor sticky with sugar. "They waste so much, while people are dying!" one man exclaimed after seeing the sugar. My neighbors came also. That family had two grown men, a woman and two teenagers, who were a little older than I was. We had known this family since before the war. They had come from our home town. They found a lot of material in the warehouse—more than they could carry. They made a deal with me. "If you let us put our things on your scooter, we will help you push it, since our houses are close together. And you can drive." The deal sounded really good— especially since I wouldn't have to push, and I could drive. I wanted to be a driver!

When the deal is "too good to be true," it is not a good deal. They tricked me. When we arrived home, they said, "Let's go to our home first, since our things are on the top." I had thought they were honest, but they fooled me. After they unloaded their belongings, they also took my things—the sugar and honey and everything else except the can of DDT.

"Wait a minute! This is my scooter, and this is my sugar!" I yelled at them.

"No! None of this is yours!" They refused to give me my belongings. All four brothers stood together, ready to beat me up.

"Dogs!" I chided them and walked away with can of poison in my hand. If they could have eaten that DDT, they would have taken it also. I went home and told my mother about it. She was very upset, but could not do anything about it. There was no law in the land; and people did what was right in their own eyes. People could have killed me and gotten away with it. There were no policemen there to catch criminals. The strong survived; the weak died.

"I am going to kill them!" I vented angrily to my mother, although I knew I was not capable of doing that.

"Son," she said, "Let them take it. To seek vengeance is of the devil; to be meek is of God." Mom quoted me a Buddhist proverb.

My anger was under control until they stole my ducks. I had been keeping all my ducks in a cage, but somehow they got out. They killed all of them and claimed them as their own. We could not identify the ducks, once their feathers were removed. I knew that they had not had any ducks before. But there was nothing I could do about it. People did whatever they wanted to; there were no laws to break. It was scary.

I thought of ways to get revenge. Being young and having little wisdom, I decided to put poison into the pond. Both of our families used that pond for drinking, cooking, and washing. I thought that the DDT would poison the water, and that when they drank the water, it would kill them. My plan did not work. It backfired on me. After I put DDT in the water, all the fish died, and the water became useless. We had to walk farther away to another pond to get our water. My mother told me, "Anger can destroy." She was right.

Cattle roamed in the fields. I went out and caught a yoke of oxen, a cow and a calf. These were valuable assets; they were "walking meat". We didn't have to carry them. Instead, they could carry all the baggage for our family. I brought them home and tied them up behind the house, making sure they could not drink of the water from the pond. But later some men in the village came, claimed that the cattle were theirs and took them.

"They are not yours!" I yelled angrily, as tears stung my eyes. They ignored me and walked away with my animals. Along with the rest of the villagers, my younger brother and I continued to go out and find more materials and food. Many people were killed by explosives during this time. The Communists had hidden bombs under some of the food supplies. Some Communists stayed behind and guarded their food supplies with guns, shooting anyone who came too close. I did not dare go too far from the village.

When the war was over, the people began searching for their relatives. After several days had passed, and our big brother had not yet appeared, we began to worry. The thought that he might have been killed crossed my mind many times. We had not seen him for a long time and did not know what had happened to him. After a while we assumed that he was dead. Many in the village returned to the places that had been their homes before the war. Mom said that she would not return to our home. We would wait until we heard from our older brother.

One day a man whom we did not recognize showed up at our house. He was terribly emaciated and walked with a cane. His back was slick with grease from the greasy backpack he carried on his back. He walked slowly, taking each step with care. He appeared so thin that a strong breeze might blow him down. As he walked toward us, my mother and I and the rest of us stood downstairs, trying to figure out who he was. At first we thought he was a beggar. "Heng, who is that? Let's go see what he wants," Mom said to me, her voice tinged with curiosity. We dropped what we were doing and walked to meet him. My heart sank at the sight of this man. I thought I was seeing my father's ghost. He looked just like Dad had looked before he died.

The man spoke first: "Mother!" He said. And then he wept.

"Cheang? My son?" Mom could not believe that this was her firstborn son.

"Yes, I am your son Cheang." I am not sure, but I believe that this was the first time I ever saw my mother hugging Cheang.

We lived together as a family in that same house for the next few months. With plenty of food to eat and the care of his family, Cheang was renewed like a tree budding in the springtime. He became big and strong and healthy. Cheang was bigger than the average Cambodian man. He stood almost six feet tall then, and he was only 16 years old.

With a big brother around the house, I took a subordinate position. Cambodians have an unspoken cultural tradition that when the father of the family is deceased, the older son assumes the father's authority. I was happy to be a little brother again. Cheang was a very good brother. He was intelligent, hard working and most of the time had a very strong will. Having a strong will was beneficial in such times, especially for the next few years. It helped him lead the family. I, too, possessed a strong will. But the bitterness and anger in my heart toward Communists almost got me in trouble.

CHAPTER 23

Hunting for Communists

With enough food and plenty of time on our hands, some of the men of the village and I formed a group to hunt for Communists. We didn't have much in the way of weapons, but we were determined to find and destroy the Communists, even if we had to use our knives, machetes, hoes, and sticks. Communists were known to come into the village at night, disguised in civilian clothes. The Vietnamese soldiers guarded each village during the day, but at night they congregated in the central compound for protection, and the villagers had to see to their own safety. The villagers said that Communists came to dig for their hidden treasures. At night we hid ourselves in the bushes, waiting for the Communists to enter the village. We were there to "welcome" them. I am thankful that I never had the opportunity to kill any of them. As much anger as I had then, I could have killed them with my own hands, but I didn't.

One evening the news spread among the villagers that two Communists, disguised as villagers, were coming into the village. They had hidden their guns and ammunition in bags on an ox-cart and were walking behind it. The men in the village held a quick meeting and divided themselves into groups. They agreed to lie in wait and capture the Communists alive. They scattered and hid in the bush and waited. I hid in a banana bush next to the house. I was scared. Darkness came. It was so dark that I could not see my hand when holding it in front of my face. I held a machete firmly in my hands, ready to strike at whatever moved. The ox-cart came into the village, and the chase began. I heard villager's loud voices.

"There!"

"Here!" Then gunshots interrupted the shouts. Light flashed from gun barrels. I was more frightened than brave and stood frozen in the banana bush with my sharp machete at the ready. "We caught one!" A shout cut through the darkness. I was standing 50 yards from the street, but could see nothing.

"The other Communist ran away!" a man shouted.

They lit torches and assembled on the street. In front of them was their prize, a young boy who looked not much older than I, with his hands tied behind his back and his head bowed forward. The gang of men pushed him forward. Some kicked him from behind. He stumbled and fell to his knees, but a man jerked the string behind him and pulled him back up onto his feet. Fear came back to me. Just a few months before I had been in his situation. For a moment I sympathized with him, but my calloused heart found no mercy. The memory of my father's desperate condition, his starvation and death came to mind and fueled the fire of my bitterness. The desire for vengeance ruled my heart. I wanted him to have no mercy; I wanted "An eye for eye, tooth for tooth, blood for blood." The mob led him away and executed him. I did not go with them to see how he was killed. But the next day I saw his body on the road. Except for a red scarf around his neck, he was naked. I am thankful that I did not join the villagers that night but instead went home and went to bed.

The next day I went fishing with the villagers at a creek, half an hour's walk from home. We used an uncommon fishing style; instead of using fishing rods, reels, hooks and lines, we all got into the water and walked back and forth, feeling the bottom of the creek with our hands and feet. The fish would get scared and lie still on the bottom. Once we felt one, we caught it.

Not long after I got there I caught a big mud fish. A mud fish looks like an alligator, but has a shorter snout. I took the fish to the shore, fastened it to my stringer, tied the stringer around my waist and got back into the creek to join the other villagers.

A young man in black shorts, shirtless like me and not much older than I, approached me and whispered, "Comrade. Do you want to live?"

I was stunned by the question and reluctantly said, "Yes."

He looked straight into my eyes and said, "If you give me that fish, I will tell you a secret." *What secret could this man tell me that would help me to live?* I wondered.

I unwrapped the stringer from my waist and handed him the mud fish. After taking his prize he motioned me to the shore with his head, and I followed. On the bank of the creek he led me to a pile of clothes on the grass. He bent over and pulled the clothes up halfway and exposed weapons—AK-47s, hand grenades and several magazines of bullets. Then he replaced the black clothes to cover the weapons.

A Communist, I thought. Should I expose him to the villagers, or should I try to kill him by myself? He could be the Communist that escaped the mob last night. His voice interrupted my thoughts. "Tonight your village and all the villagers will be destroyed. Your villagers killed one of our comrades last night, and tonight they will pay for it. So go home and take your family out so that you will be safe."

I ran home as fast as I could and told my mother and brothers about the man's prediction. Quickly we spread the news to our neighbors—even those we hated. Everyone in the village heard the news and got ready to leave. Our family packed as much rice and salt and meat as we could carry on our backs. Some villagers chose to leave the village early. West was the direction of safety. Communists occupied the territory east of us. One of our neighbors kindly allowed us to put our belongings on his wagon. But he decided to wait and see if what I told him was the truth. My reputation was on the line. I was in an awkward spot. I didn't want the people to think that I was telling them a story, but neither did I want those Communist soldiers to destroy our village. I had done my part. What they chose to believe was their business. I had learned long before that I was responsible only for my behavior—not for that of others.

Just before sunset my big brother Cheang, who was upstairs acting as a lookout, shouted, "They're coming! Lots of them!" I ran upstairs to look. Out in the open rice field hundreds—if not thousands—of soldiers in black uniforms were walking toward us. They looked like black ants, ready to swarm over some prey.

My mom yelled, "Heng! Let's go!" The man whipped the oxen to make them run. We ran behind the wagon, heading out of town, away from the soldiers. That night we camped out in the open rice field. None of us could sleep. The wetness of the dew, the irritation of insects, and anxious thoughts about the fate of our village kept us awake. We had left most of our food supply at home. We could not build a fire to warm us up, because we were afraid they would see us. The Communists must have known somehow that the Vietnamese troops had left the village for a few days. Our village was vulnerable. The people in the village had no real weapons or military personnel for defense. We could do nothing but run for our lives.

The next day we reloaded our belongings onto the wagon and moved farther westward. We feared that the Communists might be furious enough to hunt us down. We traveled in small groups of two or three families to keep from being noticed. My family and the neighbor man's family traveled together. He had his wife and a few children. Everyone was walking behind the wagon. My responsibility was to carry my youngest brother. At first he seemed light enough, but after several miles his weight became almost unbearable. We walked westward all day and found a beautiful resting place full of mature fruit trees—a kind of oasis—an island of greenery in the middle of nowhere, a paradise, refreshing to tired bodies and spirits. A big pond was there, and we bathed in it. Then we cooked food. We picked green mangos and enjoyed their sour meat.

At dawn the thunder of artillery shells awakened us. A few miles away a small group of Khmer Rouge soldiers scurried away from the exploding shells. Vietnamese forces chased them. They ran toward our "paradise".

Our neighbor quickly hid his ox-yoke in the pond. He untied his oxen and sent them off with a slap on their rumps. "Let's go!" He commanded. "Don't bring anything. The Khmer Rouge will be here any second, and we must run now!"

Everyone got up and started running. I picked Thong up, hoisted him to my shoulders and followed the crowd. We exited the paradise opposite the direction from which the Khmer Rouge were coming. We ran into the rice field and hoped that we could outrun them.

They saw us and ran toward us. Shells exploded behind them. They scurried behind a dike to protect themselves from the explosions. They kept moving toward us instead of going into the bush. More shells exploded randomly behind and around them. Then they began to chase us. All the villagers, including my mother and brothers, were well in front of me. "Hurry, Heng!" the neighbor man yelled. I tried to keep up with them, but the weight of my brother made me fall behind.

The Khmer Rouge crouched behind a dike when they heard a shell coming. After it had exploded, they got up and ran again. Everyone in my group jumped across the creek like deer. They all made it. But when it came to my turn to jump, I could not make it. I fell into the middle of the creek, and my feet sank into the mud. The water was above my head. Thong was still on my shoulders. I struggled like a trapped animal to break free from the mud, but could not. I had no more air in my lungs. Panic-stricken and in pain, I tossed Thong off my shoulders and struggled again to free myself from the mud. It seemed that the harder I struggled, the deeper I sank into the mud. With all my might I kicked against the mud with one leg, and it finally let go of me. As soon as my head rose above the water, I gasped for air, searched for Thong and glanced quickly to see where the enemies were. Thong was safely on the bank of the creek. The Khmer Rouge soldiers were just a few hundred feet away. I grabbed Thong by the hand, pushed him over the dike and rolled over after him.

"Close your eyes," I told Thong as we hid there. I didn't want him to see what would happen to us. I lay on top of my brother to protect him, expecting to be shot at any moment. We waited and waited, but nothing happened. The shells stopped exploding, and all grew quiet. I peeked over the dike, expecting to see the soldiers standing over us. But they were heading off in a different direction. I lay on my back and began to cry, realizing how close I had come to dying. The rest of my family was hiding in the same field, just a few hundred feet away.

Once the Khmer Rouge had gone and we felt it was safe to get up, we went back to the paradise to gather our belongings. Our neighbor said, "We are too far away from the village. We don't have the protection of the Vietnamese soldiers. We must move closer to town to get their protection." The next day we moved to a village that was closer to our home. Another shootout was taking place in our village, and we couldn't go back yet. From the top of a tree my older brother Cheang could see that shooting and burning was happening in our town. A strong wind was blowing toward us from the village, and it brought to us the smell of burning human flesh. The shooting continued until evening.

The next day we went into our village. Fires smoldered alongside the village street, and the smell of burning flesh was strong. On one side of the street three large trucks lay on their sides, completely burned. Smoke still trickled upward from one of them. One truck had been towing a big gun on a trailer. It, too had been burned. "They used this to shoot airplanes," an old man explained to me. Foxholes lined the street. On the side of one of the trucks many helmets, magazines and rifles were piled on top of each other. I crouched to look inside one of the trucks. Chunks of human flesh, mixed with blood, were scattered about its interior.

A brown box, partly hidden in a little bush some distance away, caught my attention. I went to it and carefully picked it up. It was quite heavy. I opened it. It was full of hand grenades. They were still good; the safety rings were still in place. I closed the lid and took the box with me. I walked over to a pile of guns on the grass. They had black ashes on them. A few other men were looking at them also. I set the box of grenades down and kicked the guns to shake off the ashes. I picked up one of the guns to inspect it. The magazine was still in it, but it was empty. One of the men said, "They are all burned. You cannot use them."

"What a waste!" I replied and tossed the useless gun into the grass. I continued to search for weapons, but found none, except a few live bullets. I put the bullets into the grenade box and went home to look for my family.

CHAPTER 24

The Ruins of War

Mom and Cheang and the rest of my brothers were inspecting the ground where our home used to be, when I caught up with them. The house and everything in it—all the food and clothes—was gone, burned down to the ground. The ashes were still smoldering. With our bare feet we kicked over black fragments of burnt wood, but found nothing. Our hope was gone. Our food supply and everything we needed for life was gone. They were irreplaceable. The white building was empty. We were homeless. Such a short time ago we had feasted. Now we were in a famine and had no place in which to live. Life in a torn world was not predictable. It was either feast or famine.

We were discouraged, but we did not completely lose our spirit, our will to live. Our family moved to a little village named Poy Ta Sak, a few miles west from our burned-out home. We lived under the trees with other homeless families. Several of the people in the community banded together to look for food in distant villages. It was dangerous, because the Khmer Rouge were hiding in some of the villages. Cheang and I risked our lives and went with these bands. We did find some rice, which we brought back to the family. But some were not so fortunate. They stepped on land mines that were buried in the ground or in the grain. Some were injured badly, and some died. Because of these horrors, our mother forbade us to go. For the next few months our family lived on grain gleaned from the rice fields. From sunrise to sundown everyone in our family went out to the fields to glean rice.

One morning, when we were on out way to the fields, a middle-aged man walking opposite us with a hoe on his shoulder recognized my mother. "Say Guech?" he inquired of my mother.

"Yes!" My mother hesitated. "Who are you?" She did not recognize him. In a starving and worn-down country people age more quickly than in a country that has food and peace.

"I am Po, from your father's village," he said.

"Oh, Uncle Po! These are my children—Cheang, Heng, Meng and Thong." The man nodded as she pointed her finger at us, from the oldest to the youngest. "Have you heard anything about our town, Uncle Po?" Mom was desperate to hear news about her brothers and sisters.

"No. But where is your husband?" he said, changing the subject.

"He is dead from starvation." Mom sadly informed him.

"Where do you live?" He asked Mom. Our mother informed him of our unfortunate circumstances.

"Why don't you and your children come and stay in my house?" he invited. "It is not much of a house—only a little thatch roof on a dirt floor. But there is plenty of room for both your family and mine." Mom reluctantly accepted his invitation. She wanted to preserve our family honor by not giving the wrong impression to the villagers. But because Mr. Po was a friend of the family and old enough to be her father, Mom thought it would be appropriate for us to accept his invitation.

On the day we moved into his house we found out that his wife and children were temporarily separated from him. He did not tell us why, and we didn't ask, assuming that it must have something to do with the war. We continued gleaning grain and lived at Po's house for the next few months. It was nice to have a roof over our heads after a long day of labor. Our family was very grateful for his generosity.

Suddenly, with no apparent cause, Mom said that we had to move out of Po's house. Without a place of shelter, we moved back into the community beneath the trees. A few days after we moved there Mom told me the reason why we had had to move. "Po insulted me, son!" she said.

"What are you saying Mom? What did he do to you?" I was angry.

"That dirty old man said that he loved me and wanted me."

"What?" I exploded like a volcano. "I am going to kill that dirty old man!" I promised my mother. I ran over to fetch my machete, which was leaning against a tree. With the sharpening stone I honed its blade to a razor edge. I tested the blade to see if it would shave hair from my leg. It did. "Cheang," I called to my big brother, "bring your machete with you and come with me. I am going to kill Po."

"What? Why?"

"That dirty dog, Po, insulted our mother and our family. While we were gone in the field, he did something bad to Mom." I snapped with anger. "He wanted to sleep with her. He told Mom that he loved her, but Mom told him no. That dirty old man deserves to die, and I am going to see to it that he does!" I ran toward Po's house. I had never killed anyone before, but I was determined that Po would be my first victim.

When we arrived at Po's house, he was inside, but as soon as he saw me, he pulled his door closed and locked it. "Open the door! Come out to face me like a man, old man!" I yelled at him through the door. "I am going to kill you, old man! No one will insult my mother! You have a wife. Sleep with her!" I pulled his door with one hand but it was locked. I ran around the house to see if there were any openings, but there were none. Cheang was calm, but I was in a rage. After running around a few times without success, I warned him, "If you ever come close to my mother, I will kill you!"

"Come on, Heng, let's go back home," Cheang said. He always seemed to be calmer than I. Mom said that Cheang had a strong will, but this time he chose not to show it. It would have been better for me to save my energy for what lay ahead instead of getting so upset, but I felt good about confronting Po. I needed to prove to myself that I was no longer a boy, but a man, a thirteen-year-old man.

Mom knew that our family needed to find shelter; the monsoon season was coming soon. By this time many people had moved back to their home towns. Kendal, our hometown, was more than two hundred miles away. It would take us months to walk there in the summer heat. Mom decided against going there, and distance was not the only reason. She said that she didn't want to go back home, because it would bring back painful memories. Also she did not know whether any of our relatives were living. She thought that they were probably dead, and that home would not be home without them.

Because of this Mom went to a man named Sun, the leader of a village called Au Ngor, to see if he could find us a place to stay before the winter rains came. He found us an abandoned home in his village. Our family shared it with another widow lady and her little boy. Her husband had been killed by the Khmer Rouge, because he was a professor.

CHAPTER 25

The Farm

The Khmer Rouge Communists had been forced into the jungle, and the Vietnamese controlled Cambodia. The government gave us barley rations. None of us had eaten this before, so we began to look for food on our own. We searched in other villages and in the forest to find hidden food supplies. The Communists hid bombs in the food. Every day people were killed. The Khmer Rouge were like devils. They wanted to steal and to destroy innocent life. Because of this danger Mom did not want us boys to go very far to search for food. She began to talk to us about growing our own food. Why not? We knew how to do it. The only problem was that we had no land, no oxen, no plow, and—most importantly—no seed. But we believed that if we worked hard, we could have a farm.

An old man named Grandpa Plong took pity on us and gave us four acres of land. He was a man of good character, a native of the village. He and his wife had several fine children. The plot of land was located several miles away from the village. Grandpa Plong's land was next to a creek. Ours was on the opposite side of the field.

First we had to prepare the ground. The ground was hard, and we had neither oxen nor plow. Early each morning all five of us packed our barley lunch and walked to the field, arriving before the sun rose. Using hand tools, we tried to get as much done as we could before noontime. The afternoons were hot and humid. Cheang acted as if he were a general in the army. He measured the land with his steps. He used sticks to mark off four equal lots and assigned one to each of us to till. Little brother Thong stayed under the shade of a tree and watched us.

From morning until dark we each worked with a hoe to break the ground in our lots. As the ground was broken, our hands broke open with blood and blisters. But Cheang encouraged us not to quit. After several days we had tilled only one acre of ground. The task seemed impossible. Our bodies got weaker, because we did not have time to look for food.

I took a little time to fish with a spear and a fishing pole, but caught only a few fish. Then an idea came to me. The hand grenades—I could kill fish with them! I took them to the creek. Pulling one out of my pocket, I carefully held it in my right hand and pulled out the safety ring with my left, as I had seen a soldier do during one of the battles. I quickly tossed the grenade into the creek, then ran and hid behind a palm tree. The grenade exploded, blasting water high into the air. I stood on the bank and watched to see if any fish would turn belly-up. Sure enough, a few small fish came wiggling to the surface, with their bellies up. I took off my clothes and dove into the water to collect my prize. Big fish came up, too, but they were stronger than the little ones. When I tried to grab them, they struggled and slipped away. One hand grenade killed enough fish for only one meal. It was not a good trade, but better than having no food. The old fishing proverb—"Give a man fish, and you feed him for a day. Teach a man how to fish, and you feed him for a lifetime."—may work with rod and reel, but not with hand grenades! I fished this way several times, but kept a few grenades for the protection of our family. I have heard of people protecting their homes with shotguns. I protected mine with hand grenades. I figured that if a burglar tried to rob us, I would hand him a grenade. I waited for such an opportunity, but it never came.

I must confess that I did some things with them that I should not have done. I hid one of them in my mother's rice bucket. When she found it, she yelled, "Help! Someone help me! There is a bomb in my rice!" She frightened the whole town. I quickly removed the bomb and confessed that it was I who had placed it there. She scolded me harshly.

Another mean idea came to me. There was a wedding in the village, and I was not invited. They had prepared food and set it out for their guests. I just happened to walk by. There was a big crowd in the house, witnessing the wedding ceremony. "Why do people have time for love and weddings while other people are starving?" I could not understand their motive. The aroma of food caught my attention. It smelled so good! I wanted to eat it. I did a terrible thing, something that no bride or groom could forgive. I stopped their wedding with a hand grenade. I tied a grenade to a tree behind their house. Then I tied one end of a string to the safety ring and the other end to a tree, as I had seen the Communists do. I ran into the house and shouted, "Bomb! There's a bomb outside!" People panicked. The wedding stopped. The people scurried outside. I went into the kitchen and ate their food. When I had eaten all wanted, I went back outside, disarmed the grenade and walked away with a full stomach. It was a bad act. But I made it up to the family later.

Many times thoughts of revenge came into my heart. I was tempted to throw a grenade into the house of the family who had stolen the three-wheeled scooter from me. That would have shown them who had more power! But I did not do it. Killing people was an ultimate sin. And if I killed, then I was no better than the killer Communists. But I was quite sure that if I saw a Communist who was responsible for the death of a member of my family, I would not hesitate to pull the safety pin and blow him up. We all did what seemed right in our own eyes. We lived like animals, governed not by moral or legal standards, but by hunger.

Our field looked too big for our family to till with hand tools; the task seemed impossible. It was like trying to cross the ocean in a canoe. We worked several days and tilled only half of the land. The monsoon was due to begin at any time, and our soil was not yet ready for planting. As we sat under the tree, taking a few moments' refuge from the scorching afternoon sun, we looked at the unfinished land and felt helpless. Grandpa Plong and his children had already finished with their tilling, and his farm was ready to receive seed. Grandpa Plong had compassion on us. He allowed us to use his oxen and plow to finish the last acre. Cheang and I took turns plowing. He was big and strong enough to control the oxen and plow handle. I was not. We finished just in time to sow seeds before the monsoon hit.

The rains came right on time. All we could do was hope that the rice seeds would grow. Day after day Cheang and I worked to keep weeds out of the rice paddies, taking short times of rest in the shade of a tree. Sometimes we went out looking for food, fishing with hand grenades, catching frogs, hunting for rats and snakes. We ate whatever we could catch.

One day as Cheang and I were walking on the dike, a snake about an inch in diameter and several feet long ran across our path. The snake got scared. It dodged this way and that as I tried to catch it. Suddenly it dived into a shallow hole in the dike, leaving half of its body sticking out. I grabbed it by the tail and tried to pull it out, but it would not budge. "Help me pull this snake out!" I shouted to Cheang. Together we tugged at the snake as if playing tug of war. Finally the snake's body separated from its head. Cheang and I had snake meat for lunch.

Like any brothers, Cheang and I had our disagreements. Late one afternoon Cheang sent me home to get lunch and told me not to be gone long. But when I got home, Mom wanted me to eat before returning to the field. Wanting to be a good son, I obeyed Mom, but when I returned to the field, Cheang ran toward me like a leopard chasing prey, churning up dust as he went. I thought he was glad to see me, but he was hungry and angry. We had a boxing match. I ended up crying.

We devoted most of our time to farming, and the rest to hunting food. It was a bad year for farming; the rains stopped early, and we had a drought. A few showers came early in the season, and then it got really dry. Famine came to Cambodia. Crops turned brown. Farmers abandoned their crops and looked elsewhere for food.

A few people in our village got together and planned to go to Thailand to look for food. Such a trip would be very dangerous. They had to go through jungles filled with traps, snakes, land mines and—worst of all—Communists. The Khmer Rouge soldiers had made their home in the jungle. They dug holes in the ground, set sharp, poison-tipped sticks in them and covered the holes with leaves. Rumors spread that the jungle was so dangerous, few people could make it through alive. The idea frightened me. I was prepared to do whatever necessary to avoid going into the jungle.

Cheang and I decided that, instead of going through the jungle, we would see to it that our rice crop did not die. We watered our field by carrying buckets of water from the creek. The water we poured onto the field seemed to evaporate quickly. We were the only two people out there in the field doing this. We carried water all day and into the night to save our crops. The effort paid off. We saved three-fourths of our crop.

Harvest time was still a ways off. In the meantime, our family became very desperate for food. We had to make a difficult decision. Mom decided to send Cheang into the jungle with her wedding ring, so that he could trade it for food. I could see that in this case it was to my advantage not to be the firstborn son. Cheang went with a number of men from our village. We were afraid for him, and there was nothing we could do but wait. I spent most of my time alone at the farm.

Something extraordinary happened during that time. I have to believe that God sent help when we so desperately needed it. Two big wild dogs, one tan, one brown, came running toward me while I was working on the farm. Dogs were rarely seen during the famine, because people ate them. These dogs were fat and strong. At first I was afraid of them and ran toward a tree, thinking I might need to climb out of their reach. But the dogs acted friendly as they approached me. They wagged their tails and did not growl or bark. I didn't know what to do. At first I thought that I should kill them for food. But I did not know how I would do that. Their playful movements disarmed me, and my fear disappeared. They nodded their heads at me and turned away, acting as if they wanted me to follow them. At first I didn't understand, but then I followed them. They led me to a small bush by the creek, where I had fished before. They went into some brush that was several feet tall. They barked and jumped up and down and suddenly one of them tossed a big rat up into the air. He killed it by biting its head and dropped it in front of me. The rat was still warm, and blood was dripping from it when I picked it up. The dogs hunted rats for me. They brought me twenty rats that day. After they finished their hunt, they came closer to me, looked me straight in the eyes, then turned and ran into the field and disappeared.

I didn't know what to think. People would not believe me if I told them what happened. The villagers would call me a lunatic and maybe kill me. For a long time I wondered where those dogs came from. Years later I read in the Bible about how God sent a raven to feed one of his prophets. I am not saying that I am a prophet, but I believe that God sent those dogs to rescue my family and me in a desperate time.

Cheang was gone for more than two weeks. Some of the people with whom he had gone had already returned. Mom began to worry. She and I went around to ask if anyone had seen him. Finally he showed up. To our surprise, he brought nothing with him, but we were overjoyed at seeing him alive.

"Cheang, Son, where have you been?" Mom inquired.

Cheang reluctantly told his story. In a small town near the jungle he had observed a gambling session—a game called "three cards." Two of the cards were queens, and one was a spade. If a person picked the queen, he won, but if he picked the spade, he lost. Cheang saw this as a great opportunity and gambled with his mother's ring. He lost. That's why he didn't bring anything with him. He did not go into the jungle. I think maybe God used that to spare his life. The jungle was very dangerous.

CHAPTER 26

Through the Jungle

We still needed food. I did not like the idea, but Mom wanted to send me into the jungle. Mom thought that at the age of thirteen I was big and mature enough for such a responsibility. Otherwise, she would not have sent me. I was fearful, but also somewhat excited about the possibility of adventure.

With a day's supply of rice and rat meat packed in a cloth bag called a "krama", and with a small knife fastened at my waist, I left home and walked toward the towns of Monkol Barai and Sway Si Sam Pon. Mom said that at Sway Si San Pon I could ask people for directions on how to get to "Ou"—Cambodian for a place in Thailand. Mom gave me a few half-dollar sized silver coins. One side of each coin had the image of the Statue of Liberty on it. The other side had some French words that I could not understand. "Buy sugar or anything that is light for you to carry," Mom instructed me.

I guarded those silver coins with great care. I saw the gamblers, and hatred for those crooked cheaters burned inside of me. I ate all my food on the first day, because I was very hungry. Also I figured that I could run faster with the food in my stomach than I could with a dangling bag.

That night at Sway Si San Pon I snooped around to see if anyone else was planning to go through the jungle. I did not know how to go through the jungle. All I knew about it was that it was dangerous, difficult and scary. I heard that groups could hire a guide to take them through, but this required a large fee of gold that I didn't have. I was like a lost puppy—scared and desperate. But I felt I must go to Thailand. My family needed my help. "I can do it." I told myself, trying to get psyched up for it.

I was learning that life often brings unwelcome responsibilities, and I must accept them, because they are good for me. I also learned that challenges always seem bigger than they really are, but one cannot know the truth about them until he sees them face to face. That night I happened upon a group about fifty men who were huddling together, making plans to cross the jungle. Because I was a kid, they paid little attention to me, and I eavesdropped on their meeting. I did not hear much of what was said, but I did understand that they planned to leave early in the morning, and they were to follow one another's steps. I decided to tag along with them. I figured that because the group was so large, no one would notice me. And if they did, I would just follow them at a distance.

The group woke up at two o'clock in the morning and left. A half moon was all we had to light the way. The cold November wind reminded me that I needed more on my body than the shorts and short-sleeved shirt I wore. We walked through forests and then open fields. I felt cold dew on my skin and face. I untied the Krama from around my waist and wrapped it around my head to keep warm. Then we came into swampland. With each step I could feel the mud pulling at my feet. Sometimes I feared that I would be left behind. The group traveled at a brisk pace. Somehow I kept up with them. We were in swampland for several hours. My legs grew tired of fighting against the mud. It felt as if I were walking through glue.

Just before the dawn we entered the jungle. Only then did the group stop and rest for a few minutes. I was so happy to feel dry ground again. The swamp had worn me out. I savored the moment. So far no one had noticed me. It was still dark, and our bodies and faces were smeared with mud.

I found out what the group leader meant when he had said, "Everyone must follow everyone else's footsteps." Following instructions in this case was a matter of life or death. After resting, the group lined up in single file. I chose to be last in line so that no one would recognize me. We all placed our feet in the footsteps of the person in front of us. At first it seemed only a bit awkward, but after a few hours my neck and legs ached with weariness. We had to walk that way in order to avoid stepping on land mines or traps.

When we first entered the jungle, the trees were small, and sunlight could reach the ground. But as we moved farther into the jungle, the trees were larger, and thick foliage prevented the sunlight from reaching us. I was thankful that I had found these people. With the people in front of me, the jungle that I once feared was not as bad as I had thought it would be. I did pass one place where a trap was exposed, and I saw that my foot was only an inch from slipping into it! For a moment my heart seemed about to leap out of my chest. The poisonous traps and landmines were placed there up by the Khmer Rouge to protect themselves. They also patrolled the jungle and would shoot anyone they considered a threat.

My sense of hearing was enhanced in a time of fear. The call of a bird or the cracking sound of a squirrel startled me and distracted me from placing my foot in the right spot. The thought of the land-mines and poisonous bamboo sticks beneath my feet was equally distracting. We traveled half a day without stopping. My throat was parched, and my legs ached, but I had to keep going. No water was in sight. We climbed a mountain. Each step brought pain to my legs. To quench my unbearable thirst, I sucked on wild bamboo. It tasted bitter.

The journey went better than I expected. I was in "the most dangerous jungle in the world," and yet I was still alive. Finally we stopped to rest. Everyone had food to eat except me. I had eaten mine the previous day. I ate more of the bitter bamboo shoots. I was hungry but happy to be alive. After a short rest, we moved on in silence, and at a very fast pace. We began to climb again. My calf muscles were stretching, and I began to think I might not make it. Pain came from my feet and legs and chest. But somehow I kept up with the rest, even though I was the youngest in the group. It was much easier when we ran downhill. When darkness fell, and we could no longer see our way, we stopped and rested. It was totally dark in the jungle at night. No fires were allowed. We camped by a small puddle of muddy water. I tried to drink some, but ended up with more mud than water in my mouth.

The men huddled together and rested. With a tree trunk as a pillow and a shield against the threat of a shootout, I slept sitting up. We had neither a campfire to warm us nor food to eat. No one was allowed to light a match or to smoke. The Khmer Rouge might see us. Cold and scared, I listened as the men talked in low tones about what the next day would bring. That was even more terrifying. But somehow I fell asleep.

The next day we journeyed at an even faster pace. We ran constantly. That made it much more difficult to follow each other's footsteps. The group leader demanded silence. He warned us that in this area there was a greater concentration of land mines and booby-traps, and many Khmer Rouge soldiers. Adrenaline was pumping high, and energy I did not know I possessed strengthened my legs and feet. I kept up with the group. I was determined not to be left behind. I knew that if I were alone, I would die in the jungle. Along the way I saw the dead bodies of those who had fallen into the traps. This encouraged me to keep on running.

Pain seared my chest, and my throat was dry. I had to remember that I was running for my life and for my brothers and my mother. I was quite sure that I wanted never to go through this again! After running for half a day, we stopped and rested. Again there was no water.

The guide was short and dark and square-faced, with a pronounced lower jaw. A man of few words, he would have made a good training sergeant in the army. He gathered the group together and whispered some instructions that I could not hear. Not knowing what was ahead made me nervous, but I figured I would do all I could to keep up with the others. The group had paid this guide to take them through the jungle, and I had not. To him and the rest I was a parasite, and they were not obligated to tell me anything. I was grateful that they didn't kill me. I was very careful not to cause them any trouble.

As we rested, I sat next to the only man who would talk with me during the journey. He took a wad of paper from his pocket and showed it to me. I recognized that the papers were currency, but did not know to which country they belonged. Each bill had a man's picture on it, but I did not know who they were.

"These are dollars!" He said, "U.S. money!"

"What is U.S.?" Being uneducated, I had never heard of that country.

He smiled and said, "A Kang!"

"Oh," I answered, understanding at last. "They are the people who caused our country to be at war. They are our enemies."

He nodded his head in agreement. These bills were more precious than gold or silver, because the Thai people knew the value of dollars. Robbers in the jungle didn't. Yes, there were robbers everywhere in the jungle. They traveled in large groups and carried many weapons. Some were Cambodian, and some Thai. They robbed anyone they could find in the jungle. They were merciless. They would force men and women to strip off their clothes before they executed them. I marveled that people could be so cruel, but then I remembered Hitler and Pol Pot.

When people refuse to believe that there is a God, and that He created them, they think that life is an accident and has little value. Because they don't believe that a Supreme Power will judge them, they think that evil actions will go unpunished, and they do whatever seems right to them—even to the point of killing others. Before he died, Pol Pot said that his conscience was clear. He had no remorse over having killed half the population of Cambodia. People can be terribly cruel. Our guide told us that within the next hour we would encounter such people. We rested so that we could run for the next several hours.

"Let's go!" The guide got up and signaled us to follow him. "Run fast, and keep your head down," he whispered. "We will cross the Khmer Rouge's Number One firing line in one hour." This was the most dangerous area in the whole jungle. Khmer Rouge soldiers patrolled this line to protect their territory. We needed to cross the line when they were not present. There were two more patrol lines—Number Two and Number Three. With head and shoulders held low, we started to run. When we came close to Line Number One, we stopped and sat down. Our guide crawled forward on his belly forward to investigate the line. Finding it safe, he motioned with his hand for us to follow him. Like alligators we crawled on our bellies and elbows to meet him.

Then we stood up and began to run again. We crossed the line without seeing a Communist.

The line was nothing more than a well-worn footpath. On either side of it the trees and brush had been cut down so that the soldiers could see people coming. Suddenly, just as I was crossing the line, I saw a flash of sunlight reflecting from liquid in a foxhole off to my left. *Water!* I thought. And then I did a stupid thing; I obeyed my thirst. I stopped, knelt down and scooped up water with both hands and drank it quickly. Immediately I regretted what I had just done. I felt something slimy in my mouth. I spat it back out with a cough, and rotten, fatty flesh came out. I looked into the foxhole and was shocked to see a dead, rotting body, floating face down in it. I gagged and ran back toward the group.

A shower of bullets spattered around me. The Khmer Rouge had seen me! I ran in a zigzag pattern to throw off their aim. Bullets whistled past me, but I kept on running. I felt no pain. Even after the shooting stopped, I kept on running until I caught up with the group. I checked my body for bullet holes, but did not find any. God had protected me. But I still felt and tasted the horrid stuff that was in my mouth. And I couldn't wash it out; there wasn't any water.

Line Number Two and Line Number Three were all clear, but we did not linger; we ran quickly across these danger zones. We ran for several miles after crossing the last line. Then we slowed to a fast walk. It took the rest of the day for us to reach a refugee camp called "Old Camp." It was located near the Thai border. Some said that the majority of people living there were families of Khmer Rouge soldiers. There were thousands of blue canvas tents there, in long rows. Hundreds of people lived outside, with no shelter at all. The sun had turned orange and was about to set when we arrived at the refugee camp. New arrivals gathered with their families along the creek. There was a flurry of activity; people were trying to get last-minute details done before darkness fell. I stayed close to my group.

A sense of safety and celebration had come over me as I stepped into the camp, but it was quickly replaced by fear when I found out that the people in this camp were really Khmer Rouge—fugitives from the current government in Cambodia. This was their hideout! I was in the eye of the tiger. Our lives were in danger.

When we reached the creek in the middle of the camp, our guide spoke to us. "We will stay here and rest for a few hours. Don't drink any of this water. It is contaminated with sewage. Tonight we will enter a Thai village and trade. Tomorrow we will head back toward our village." He sat down and rested.

You don't have to warn me twice about contaminated water, I thought as he spoke. Then I began to wonder how I would trade. *How would I communicate with the Thai people?* After it had been dark for some time, we left the camp and went into the Thai village. Many refugees went with us. I clutched my four precious silver coins in my right hand. We entered a small house that sat on stilts. Several men sat cross-legged on the floor. To my surprise, one of them spoke my language—Khmer.

"What do you have to trade?" he said to me.

"Four silver coins, sirs!" My voice trembled. I had lived through almost four years of silence under the Khmer Rouge regime, and my conversation skills had suffered.

He snatched my precious coins as if they had no value and spoke without a hint of compassion. "One hundred barts," he said, as he handed them back to me.

"Yes, sir," I agreed, handing the coins back to him. One hundred sounded good. I did not know what a reasonable exchange would be. I knew only that I needed to buy food for my starving family.

With one hundred barts clenched in my fist, I followed the group into the Thai market, which was situated in an open field. Twenty-five pounds of rice, five pounds of sugar and a box of ramen noodles—that was all I could buy with 100 barts. A snow cone was very appealing to me on such a hot summer evening, but I had no money left. All I could do was to observe as others ate and drank. That night, before crossing back to Cambodia, I ate a package of ramen noodles.

CHAPTER 27

The Journey Home

The journey home went much slower. The weight of the food on our shoulders made us tire more quickly, and we rested more often. At first the thirty pounds of precious, life-saving material on my shoulders didn't seem like much, but after several hours the weight became almost unbearable. I shifted it from one shoulder to the other and sometimes placed it on the top of my head to give my shoulders a rest. We saw no Communists, but we knew that we might at any time. We saw several fresh bodies along the way. The Khmer Rouge could not be far away. We were not safe.

Following each other's footsteps became very difficult as our burdens brought pain to our shoulders and back. The days were hot and humid, and there was no breeze. Birds, startled at the sight of us, made a frightful racket. I wanted to wring their necks and silence them.

A cold chill quivered through my spine, and I became weaker. That which I feared most had came upon me; I was getting sick. I didn't want to be left alone in the jungle. It seemed as though the group was walking faster and faster; the back of the person in front of me moved farther and farther ahead. I could not keep up with the pace. The chill got worse; my teeth chattered against each other. I knew that something was seriously wrong with me, and I began to pray for the grace of my mother and father and grandparents. *"Please, help me,"* I prayed silently. But I got worse. My knees wobbled like those of an infant learning to walk. Fear enveloped me. The group did not slow down. They seemed not to notice. I didn't blame them; they had their own burdens to carry, and to them I was a stranger.

No one could survive alone in the jungle—especially one who has malaria. I had no defense against wild animals, robbers or Communists. My legs wobbled. I could not pick up my feet to take another step. I wanted to cry out to the group and ask them to wait, but I didn't. Weeping, I crept off the path and crawled into a jungle thicket to hide. Rain fell. I was cold. Chills went down my spine. I broke off a few leaves and wrapped them around my package in a feeble effort to keep it dry. I dragged it behind me as I crawled. Some two hundred feet off the path I found a tree with a hole in its trunk. I placed the food package inside and used it as a pillow. I was able to get about half of my body inside. A hole like this would usually be a good sanctuary for snakes, but now it was my hiding place. No one could find me. *I will die here*, I thought. I wrapped my arms around my body like a blanket to keep myself warm and lay there in a fetal position. My jaw was clenched tight to keep my teeth from chattering, and my head throbbed with a piercing headache.

I felt that, for me, time was running out. Questions raced through my mind. *Is there a God? If so, where is He? What will happen to me when I die? Is heaven a real place, as people say it is?* I knew that I had done bad things. *Could a man who had done bad things go to a perfect place called heaven? What about that place people called hell?* I didn't want to go there! I prayed a prayer that I had never prayed before. *"If there is a God, (and I think there must be), please hear me. I don't know who you are, but you know who I am. Please help me by protecting me. Please keep me safe. I don't want to die here alone."* Then I fell asleep.

When I awoke, the fever had broken. I must have slept several days. I was hungry. I had disciplined myself not to touch the food I was carrying, but now I opened the package and ate some ramen noodles mixed with sugar. I rationalized that the package would weigh less, and I needed the energy.

From my hideout I tried to figure out which direction to go. The sun rose from the east and set in the west, but from the floor of the jungle the sun could not be seen. I thought about climbing to the top of a tree to look for the sun, but the trees had no branches low enough to reach. Besides, I didn't want to become a target for Communists. Nor did I have strength for climbing. God must have heard my cry. Three days later a group, similar to the one that had left me, came by. I joined them and returned home. I knew then that some God had heard and delivered me. But I did not know which God it was until years later. This psalm says what I felt at that time: "I will bless the LORD at all times: His praise shall continually be in my mouth. My soul shall make her boast in the LORD. The humble shall hear thereof and be glad. O magnify the LORD with me and let us exalt his name together. I sought the LORD, and he heard me and delivered me from all my fears. This poor man cried, and the LORD heard him and saved him out of all his troubles." (Psalm 34:1) I learned from this that the Lord could deliver me out of any situation if would call on His name.

My family was happy to see me returning safely with food. But soon that small supply of food was almost gone. A new fear spread among the villagers: young men were being drafted into the army. The Vietnamese military began to require all single men sixteen years old or older to sign up. Truckloads of young men were shipped to Vietnam for military training. No one knew what happened to them. We never saw any of them return. The Vietnamese might have been telling the truth, but the villagers who had already had bad experiences with the new government were reluctant to trust it. My mother was one of those who chose not to believe. She had good reason; her oldest son Cheang was sixteen.

CHAPTER 28

A Haven Spoiled

Fear of the draft and lack of food caused my mother to conclude that our family should escape to another country. Mom asked if I would go into the jungle with her to see if the path was safe enough for the whole family.

"No, the path is not safe, and I will not go!" I was determined not go into that deathtrap again. I would rather have my leg cut off than to go through that jungle again. I figured that the worst my mother might do to me for disobeying her was to kill me. Jungle meant death anyway. What was the difference?

"Heng, if we don't escape, our family will die," Mom persuaded me. "We have no rice, and the drought is the worst in a long time. Besides, do you want them to take away your big brother?" Mom knew my weakness.

"How about returning to our home town?" I asked. "Everybody else has gone back. Why haven't we?" I tried every excuse to avoid entering that deadly jungle.

"Heng! I never want to return to our home town!" Mom spoke with a quivering voice and tears in her eyes. "I feel betrayed by our own people. They killed our family, and your father is gone. Your aunts and uncles are dead and gone. I have no reason to return. I don't want to live here in Cambodia and be reminded of their suffering and death. I want to be anywhere but here. If you don't take me, I will go by myself," she said with finality.

I, too, spoke with finality. "I am going back into that jungle!"

During the next few months a stream of Cambodians traveled in a massive exodus along the road through our village, on their way to Thailand. Political instability and starvation forced people to leave the country. Some said that the jungle was not as dangerous as it once had been. And if we were fortunate enough to make it safely through the jungle, we could go and stay in a refugee camp along the Thai border. Rumors spread that the United Nations had established a refugee camp there.

The rumor was correct. I took my mother safely through the jungle and brought her to a refugee camp called Kouk Kchoong. In the camp Mother met an old friend, who invited us to stay in her tent temporarily. The United Nations gave us plenty of rice and other foods. Mom thought that this place was a safe haven sent from God. Without hesitation she told me to go back to Cambodia to bring the rest of my brothers. I knew that I would face resistance from Cheang. He would not want to leave Cambodia. Our rice field was ready to be harvested.

"The younger brothers will do what I tell them," I told Mom, "but the big brother will be a problem."

She agreed. "Just tell Cheang that Mother wants the whole family to come to the refugee camp. Forget about the rice field. There is plenty of rice here. And it is free." My mother knew the art of convincing. She convinced me. I was not sure that Cheang could be convinced, but one catches more flies with honey than with a swatter, so I decided I would appeal to him kindly.

I left the safety of the camp with enough food to last me for a few days, but took no extra food for the brothers. This time I knew the way home. The jungle seemed smaller and less fearsome; many people were traversing it at that time. Knowing the way and knowing what to do took away most of the fear.

At dawn Mom whispered, "Heng, wake up! It is time to go, son!" I was a light sleeper, so I woke up quickly, got to my feet and got ready to leave. Mom tried to give me some last-minute instructions. I didn't listen very well, because I already knew them. "Tell your brothers to come. I'll be waiting for you here," she said.

Convincing my two younger brothers to come would be easy, but the oldest brother Cheang would be a challenge. He was an independent thinker and was not inclined to accept instruction from a younger brother. I decided that I would relay Mom's message. If necessary, I would leave him behind in Cambodia.

The jungle was much the same—hot, humid and scary. Shortly after entering into it, I came upon a caravan of people who were escaping from Cambodia to the refugee camp. One family had seven children. Two of them rode on the rear carriers of bicycles. The other five held hands as they walked. None of them looked more than ten years old. All of them were crying. They looked very malnourished—their bones showed through blackened skin. Several of them were naked.

"Sir?" I asked the man who appeared to be their father, "Is it safe on the way?"

"No," he answered. "We had a shootout in the middle of the jungle. We didn't know who shot whom. But we have not had food or water for two days. How far is it from here to the refugee's camp?"

"About a day's walk," I told the man. Just then I noticed the kids' eyes spying on my food and water supply. Their begging eyes broke my heart. "I don't have much, but here is some food and water. I gave all my food to their father.

He raised the palms of his hand as an expression of gratitude, while saying, "Thank you! Thank you so much, younger brother! May God bless you a hundredfold for your kind deed." The children surrounded their father. He carefully divided the food and gave a portion to each child, like a bird feeding its chicks. He gave a small portion to his wife, who was quietly watching.

"No," she said. "Give it to the children." The parents kept no food for themselves. They just watched their children eat.

Since that day I have given sacrificially to many people. But none of these gifts has seemed as precious as the little gift I gave to this poor family. I gave all that I had. It was special to me, because the people to whom I gave it were so desperate, and they received it with so much gratitude. Jesus was right when he said, "It is more blessed to give than to receive."

When I arrived at home, I gave my older brother the message: "Cheang, Mom told me to ask you to take our family to the refugee camp." I tried to convince him.

"No! We are not going anywhere!" Just as I thought, he was strongly opposed to the idea of moving. "Our rice farm is ready to be harvested," he continued. "We worked hard for that rice, and we will stay to reap the benefits of our labor." It was clear that he would not be dissuaded. I agreed with him. At least we should reap first, then escape.

With this agreement, all four of us brothers spent our time on the farm, chasing birds away to keep them from eating our grain. In the middle of the field we erected a scarecrow stuffed with hay. Each morning we went to the farm to inspect our crop, to see if it was ready to harvest. The grain was still too green; it had too much moisture in it. It had to turn brown or golden before we could reap it. Time seemed to drag. We learned again the truth of this proverb: "A watched pot does not boil."

A week after I returned home a stranger stopped at the house to inform us that our mother was now in Snay Si Saphn, a town about 16 miles away. The informant said, "Your mother is weak from dehydration and lack of food. She can no longer walk. She wants you to buy some food, borrow your neighbor's bicycle and come to pick her up." This was strange news. Our mother was supposed to be in the refugee camp. But the man had no reason to lie to us, so we decided that I should go and investigate.

I borrowed the bicycle, grabbed two bags of ramen noodles and rode to Sway Si Saphn as fast as I could. The man was right. I found my mother, with her head resting in the palms of her hands, sitting under a mango tree in front of a store. She looked worn out. Her body and clothes covered with mud.

"Son!" She was happy to see me.

"Mom! What are you doing here? You were supposed to wait for us in the camp." I scolded her a little, but I was feeling guilty for not returning sooner. I was expecting her to scold me for not taking my brothers to the camp as I had promised.

"Where is the food?" she asked frantically. "I have not eaten any food for several days."

"I brought two packages of Ramen noodles, Mom." I opened the bag and handed them to her. Having neither pot nor stove for cooking, Mom took the packages of noodles into the shop and asked the owner to cook the noodles for her. He cooked her one package of noodles and kept the other as payment for his service.

She thanked the man for his good deed and ate her food quickly. She climbed onto the rear carrier of the bicycle, and we rode toward home.

"So, what happened mother?" I asked, as I struggled with the pedals.

"After you left there was a shootout in the camp. I thought I would never see you again, son. Mortar shells exploded all around me, and bullets were flying everywhere. I was so frightened. I covered myself with rice bags, hoping that I would be safe. Dead bodies were everywhere. Thai soldiers came into the camp, shooting refugees and Cambodian soldiers," she said.

"I heard the shooting, Mom, but I didn't know where it was coming from," I interrupted.

"After the shooting," she went on, "I decided to come back to find you and your brothers. I could only hope that you hadn't left already. I am so glad you didn't leave."

I'm off the hook! I thought. This time I was glad I had listened to my brother.

"I was conned," She continued. "I bought two big cases of condensed milk and hired a man to carry it for me. He put them on his ox-cart and assured me that they would be safe with him."

"Condensed milk? That stuff is heavy Mom!" I interjected.

"I know! That's why I could not carry them. I walked behind him. He kept going faster and faster and wouldn't stop, even though I yelled for him to stop. I ran as fast as I could, but I couldn't catch up with him. He was a thief, Son. Everything is gone. He took them. I have not had any food for days. Son, let's go home."

"Yes, Mother!" I pedaled on. The trouble Mom had experienced in the camp washed from our minds the idea of escaping from

Cambodia. Several nearby families next door went back to their home towns. Mom sent with them a message for her brothers and sisters: we were not going back. We didn't know where would go, but we were certainly not going to either Thailand or our own home town.

CHAPTER 29

Journey to the Orphanage

People from our home town came to get members of their families. They told us that our Aunt Houy had been killed by the Khmer Rouge because of her fair skin color. Uncle Khun had been killed because of his education. To us it seemed tragic that a person should be killed for nothing more than having a certain skin color or being educated.

Our rice, the result of our hard work, was a beautiful sight as it turned golden brown. We were anxious to harvest it. But late one night Mom came back from the home of our neighbor, Mr. Kre, wearing an expression of great urgency. She gathered us together and said, "Things are not good here in our country. News has spread that the Vietnamese are still drafting young men 16 years old and older and taking them to Saigon. Also the Thai border is being closed to prevent people from escaping Cambodia. Our family cannot wait to harvest our grain. I am afraid that Cheang will be drafted, and I am determined not to have you boys taken away from me. We will have to pack and leave." Mom had made up her mind.

Cheang protested her decision. He said, "I am not going! Our farm is almost ready to be harvested. We can't leave it. We have worked very hard for it." But Mom had already made up her mind, and I agreed with her. We would pack our few belongings and secretly leave the village in the middle of the next night. The Vietnamese soldiers had tightened security in the village to keep people from escaping. Mr. Kre and a few other families would leave at the same time. He would take a yoke of oxen and a cart with him. I knew how my brother must have felt to leave the farm behind. But Mom told him to leave the farm to Mr. Plong and his family to harvest. She told Mr. Plong, "Go ahead and harvest and sell part of the grain and keep some for food. If we ever return to the village, we hope you can give us some grain. But if we never return, all the grain belongs to you." With that we left the village.

"Where is Cheang?" Mom asked anxiously. She began to run this way and that, looking for my older brother. Cheang was hiding from us. He didn't want to come with us. We found him walking far behind us. Because he was on the street, in full view of the villagers, Mom could not yell at him. Later that night she scolded him sternly for hanging back so far behind us.

We all carried loads on our backs. I carried Thong, my youngest brother. To this day I don't remember much about that trip. Mom told me that halfway through the jungle I got malaria, ran a high fever and could not walk. Mr. Kre had compassion on me. He let me ride in his ox-cart all the way to the Thai refugee camp. I woke up in a tub of ice water in the refugee camp hospital.

I stayed in the hospital for several weeks, recovering. Finally Mom took me to where she was staying. On the way we came upon an orphanage. Wars and the Khmer Rouge killings had left many children without mother or father. The orphanage was crowded. As we stood along the picket fence and watched the children play, we overheard a conversation between two ladies. One lady said, "My husband was a captain in the army. He died during Pol Pot's regime. I have four children, and I just placed them into the orphanage." She seemed proud of her husband's rank—and of her decision regarding the children.

"I heard that orphans have a better chance to get sponsored to the U.S.A.," the other lady responded. There, in the U.S., it is like heaven. All the streets are paved. There is freedom and opportunity to go to school, and plenty of good food." Her words were to my ears like raindrops to drought-stricken field.

I paid very close attention to what she said. But I was confused. I had been taught by the Communists that the U.S. was full of racial hatred and mean people. Their conversation got my mother's attention also. She asked the lady for more information. She found out that that it was a good idea to go to the U.S.A. After Mom had explained to me the advantages of going to the U.S.A., I begged her to place Meng and me into an orphanage.

A few days later a truck came to take us to a children's center in a different refugee camp. Mom tried to give us some last-minute advice before we left. Her eyes—and ours—were full of tears. She said, "Sons, I don't know if I will see you again. But if you have the opportunity to find freedom and opportunity, I want you both to keep a promise to me."

"Yes, Mother?"

"Don't forget your mother and brothers, and don't forget to study hard, work hard and pray to God to help you." These last few precious words of my mother—I have kept them in the depths of my heart. I have treasured them more than gold or silver. They have shined light on my path when I was in darkness, when I lost hope and was confused. When I was tempted to give up, these words have tugged my heart and reminded me of my responsibility and the sacrifices my mother made for me. Meng and I climbed into the back of the truck and waved good-bye to our mother. Meng was eleven years old; I was fourteen.

On that day that I made a promise to myself, to my mother and to God: I would study hard, work hard and pray to God and hope that God would allow me to meet my beloved mother and two brothers again. My heart ached as if stabbed by a knife. That day my brother and I became aliens, like our father's father. The old proverb came true for us: "The fruit does not fall far from the tree." We were headed off into the unknown, on a quest for freedom.

Many questions about the future played on the screen of my fearful mind. Emotions flooded my heart—anger against the Khmer Rouge for tearing apart my family and my country, and excitement at the prospect of going to a foreign land. I was ready to go almost anywhere—anywhere except Cambodia. With clenched teeth I pounded my fist against the side of the truck. I vowed that I would get revenge for all that my family had lost. And I would return to find my mother and brothers.

The truck left the asphalt highway and pulled onto a red clay road. Clouds of red dust rose behind us. We came to a barbed-wire gate that led into the refugee camp. A large sign, bearing the words "Khao I Dang" hung above the gate. The camp had a barbed-wire fence around it. Soon I found out that the fence was not there to keep things out; it was for keeping us in.

An armed guard came to inspect the human cargo. Then he opened the gate and stood back as the truck took us into the camp. Kao I Dang was located several miles inside the Thai border. As the truck made its way through the camp, I observed rows of the familiar blue canvas tents, stretching as far as the eye could see on both sides of the path. People—mostly women and children—stood beside the road and in front of their tents, gazing at us, studying our faces. They dropped whatever they were doing and stared at us as if we were part of a funeral procession. At first I didn't give it much thought, but after a while I began to wonder about their curiosity. Later I learned why there were so few men. Most of them were dead. The wives would say, "My husband is missing. I don't know whether he is alive or dead." Many families had children missing. Whenever new people came to the camp, they watched carefully, hoping to see a lost family member.

The caravan of trucks stopped in front of the orphanage center. A lady in her mid-fifties opened the gate. An eight-year-old girl limped along beside her. The girl wore a sarong skirt and a white t-shirt. Like the rest of us, she had no shoes. The center had four buildings, two large, two small. A sign on one of the walls said "Uneher". The lady was the orphanage superintendent. She welcomed us to the center with a smile and said, "The boys' dorm is to the right, and the girls' is to the left." Since none of us had any belongings except the shirt and pants we were wearing, unloading of the truck was accomplished quickly.

I stayed close to Meng, making sure that we found a place in the center together. We went inside one of the buildings. A row of two-foot-high beds made of bamboo strips stretched the full length of the building. I picked beds that were as far as possible from the entrance, since there would be less traffic there, and it would be quieter.

CHAPTER 30

Life in the Orphanage

My brother and I and 18 other boys were assigned to one "father". My dorm had three "fathers". Our "father" was in his early twenties, tall, handsome and well built. He had a couple of brothers who were also orphans. The second "father" was in his early thirties and had a gentle face. The third was also in his twenties, short and youthful-looking.

A bed sheet, shorts, a shirt, a spoon and a bowl were issued to us. At lunch time and supper time we brought our bowl to the cafeteria and received our rations. The food was not bad, but never enough. Sometimes for breakfast they gave us a jar of Gerber baby food. I actually developed a liking for it.

The orphanage people treated us well. In the morning all the children who were old enough were required to exercise. We did jumping jacks and jumped rope. For the rest of the morning we went to school. The school was in the middle of the camp; getting there and back required a long walk. After school we could play soccer or volleyball, learn martial arts or take lessons in traditional dance. I learned martial arts, because I wanted to know how to defend myself.

In the evening we would sometimes go to the border of the refugee camp—the barbed-wire fence—and watch the Thai soldiers patrol the camp. Refugees would sneak in and out of the camp to barter for food in the Thai villages. When the soldiers saw refugees crossing the fence or outside the camp, they would shoot them on sight—no questions asked. I watched many people get shot. I did not dare to leave the camp.

There were many orphan centers in the refugee camp. Thousands of children were waiting to be sponsored by people from different countries. But the one country that everyone wanted to go to was the United States. That was my hope and desire as well. Each morning my brother and I went to look at the bulletin board hanging on the wall of the superintendent's office, to see if our names had been listed as sponsored. Other people's names were there, but not ours. It was discouraging, but I was determined to stick with it. I disciplined myself to read and study eight hours a day in addition to the regular school curriculum. I believed that education and discipline were my ticket to the future, and all I needed was a chance to get to the United States. But getting a sponsor was hard.

Three months in the orphanage seemed like an eternity. I missed my mother and brothers. Meng made our time in the orphanage even more difficult. In the middle of the night, when everybody was sound asleep, Meng would get up, his body soaked with sweat, and kick and yell, "He's big! He's big! Help me, please, Mother!" All the children would wake up and stand around him, watching.

"What is big? Who is this, Meng?" I yelled, trying to get an answer. But he would only repeat what he had said before. He would yell like that for thirty minutes and then go back to sleep. The next day I would ask him, "What happened to you last night, Meng?"

"Nothing," he would answer. "I slept."

"You mean you don't remember anything?" I queried.

"No," he answered. And then he would run off and play with the other kids.

This happened almost every night. No one knew why this happened, but it irritated them so much that they wanted to kick us out of the orphanage. They didn't say so, but every day the other kids harassed Meng. They picked on him all the time. Meng never backed down on a verbal fight. He was good with words. But when the conflict became physical, and they began pushing and shoving him, he would run to me to rescue him. My martial arts training came in handy. Normally, we tried to find a peaceful solution, or we ran. If they chased us, I beat them up. I usually carried a mixture of sand and dry red hot pepper in my pocket. If a lot of them were chasing me, I would throw the mixture into their faces. It hurt their eyes and made it easy for me to beat them up. "Meng, you have to control yourself. Don't respond to those boys. Let them win, brother," I advised him. He argued with me, but eventually agreed. I warned him, "We can't go to America if we get kicked out of the orphanage. We must do whatever we need to in order to stay, okay? Our family's future depends on us." I tried to persuade him to be patient and good. Somehow, deep inside, I felt confident that I would go to America. And I surely didn't want anything to mess that up. For a short while things went better—until my mother showed up at the orphanage one night.

A week prior to her visit, a big shootout occurred in her refugee camp. The whole camp was enveloped in flames. We could hear rockets and guns, even though we were 20 miles away. Mom came to the orphanage center in the middle of the night, knocked on the gate and asked the superintendent to get me. My "father" woke me up and brought me to her. To prevent them from suspecting we were mother and son, we went to the gate to talk.

I was very happy to see Mother. Even though I wanted to show her how much I had missed her, I refrained from hugging her. I knew something was wrong with her, because her eyes were sad and teary. We stood outside the gate. Light from the center allowed us to see each other's faces.

"Heng, have you seen your brother Thong?" She talked with a quivering voice.

"No, Mother," I said, wondering why she had asked this.

She wept for a while. When she composed herself, she said, "Your brother, Thong, is missing. He has been missing for several weeks—ever since the shootout in the camp. I have looked every-where for him in the other camps, and he is nowhere to be found. I am going crazy. I have searched for him day and night. I have not eaten or slept."

I could hardly believe what I had heard. Missing? My four-year-old baby brother? How could he survive in the jungle? That would be like throwing a baby into a pit of crocodiles. "What happened, Mother?" I asked.

"After you left, your big brother and I started a little business to keep ourselves alive. I sold snow cones at the flea market. Your big brother was supposed to baby-sit Thong at the tent. Two weeks ago a big group of Communists came into the camp, and there was a shootout between them and non-Communists. Because he was afraid, Cheang left Thong at the tent and came to find me at the market. When we both got back to the tent, Thong was gone. He must have run away because of fear. We looked everywhere for him and could not find him. We went to the other camps and looked there, but we still have not found him. He could have fallen into a water-well and drowned. But I will not give up until I find him—dead or alive."

I was angry at Cheang for leaving Thong behind. And my heart ached for my mother and little brother. "Mom, Meng and I will start looking tomorrow," I assured her.

"But you need to get rest. Do you have a place to sleep?" I asked.

"Yes, Son. Your brother and I have a tent to sleep in only a few blocks from here, near Aunt Chek Chor's family. Do you remember her?"

"Yes, Mother, I remember her. She used to have two sons and four daughters. Her oldest son was my friend back in Cambodia. Now you go and rest, Mother. I will come to look for you in the morning," I promised. And I went back though the gate and went to bed.

For the next few months, instead of going to school, our family searched all day for Thong. We asked every living soul in the camp.

"Excuse me, have you seen a little four-year-old boy with yellow shorts?"

"No," was all we heard. We finally gave up looking for him and had to accept that he was dead. Mother began to work in the refugee hospital as a volunteer seamstress with Aunt Chek Chor. Keeping herself busy helped her cope with the loss of her son.

CHAPTER 31

Trial by Fire

Meng and I continued to live in the orphanage, but the administrators became suspicious of us. Somehow they knew that we were not orphans, and they wanted to kick us out. They never came out and said it, but they did come up with a trick.

Early one morning, "Father" yelled, "I've lost my diamond ring! I had it here last night. I am going to get married, but now it is gone." The superintendent called all the boys to a meeting in the courtyard and announced the tragedy. Out of the several hundred boys, I was the one accused of stealing the diamond ring!

"Heng! You were the only one who saw me with the ring yesterday," the accuser said.

"No, sir, I didn't know you had a ring. I did not steal it," I swore.

"You have until tomorrow to bring back the ring, or you will face the consequences," he announced in front of everybody.

"No!" I affirmed. "How can I bring back your ring if I don't have it?" I asked innocently. But my argument fell on deaf ears.

"Tomorrow! I need my ring back," was his final answer.

Shamed and embarrassed, I ran out of the center to the road and cried. I was glad that my younger brother, Meng, was not there to see me like that. I took a lot of time to think through what to do. But the thought of leaving the orphanage was not an option. *No matter what, I will stay in the center. They can do anything they want to me, but I will stay*, I said to myself. For the rest of the day

I remained silent. I avoided everyone and stayed in my bed, anxious to learn what my fate would be on the next day. I told nothing of this to Meng or to my mother. *I am a big boy*, I told myself, *and I can handle it.*

The next morning I was filled with the same sort of fear I had always felt during the Pol Pot regime. One can never get used to the companion of fear. But knowing in my heart that I was not guilty of stealing the diamond gave me enough courage to face my enemy.

In the center of the courtyard, "Father" called me. Everyone stood around, waiting to see what would become of me. They looked at me as if I were a guilty criminal on death row. I stood facing him.

"Where is my diamond ring?" He demanded. "Do you have it, Heng?"

"No, sir! I don't have your ring. If I never took it, how can I have it? Why are you doing this to me?" I talked to him as if I were a strong and determined man. "I know that you want me and my brother out of this center, but we are not going anywhere!" I stood my ground.

"Then do you swear that you didn't steal the diamond, Heng?" He seemed to back down a little.

"Yes, I swear to anything that I did not steal it." I agreed with him, but in so doing fell into his trap.

"Do you swear by fire?" He set me up. Being young and unwise, I said, "Yes, I swear by fire."

"Okay. We will put hot coals in the palm of your hand to prove that you are innocent. If you are innocent, you will not get burned, but if you are guilty, you will be burned."

Being naïve and eager to prove my innocence, I said, "Bring on the fire." Because my heart was consumed with hatred toward this man and with the desire to stay in the orphanage, I was willing to take on the challenge. He went to the kitchen and returned with a smoldering coal, which he held with a pair of metal tongs. Like an executioner, he ordered me, "Open your hand, Heng!"

With my eyes closed and my teeth clenched together, I extended my left hand toward him, palm open. Immediately I felt a burning agony in my hand. I clasped the burning coal in my hand as tightly as I could, hoping that lack of oxygen would put out the fire. The pain grew worse. I could no longer cope with it. Everyone was watching me, but I didn't care what they thought. I tossed the coal toward them, and they scurried away. I licked my hand and spat into it to cool it. I ran inside the building and poured cold water on my hand to soothe it. I crawled into bed and cried myself to sleep, with only the presence of Meng to comfort me.

They didn't kick us out of the orphanage. "What does not kill you makes you strong." The fire that burned me only strengthened my commitment to stay there. Because of my courage, and my determination to prove my innocence, people there respected me more. They let me stay in the orphanage.

Within the space of two years we were relocated to four different refugee camps. The orphanage administrators wanted the children to have the opportunity to look for their lost parents. Moving was a blessing to our family, because it helped us search for our lost baby brother, Thong. It has been said, "When you are on the bottom, the only place to look is up." So we seized every opportunity given to us. The camps were not safe. At night the foreign workers left the camp to stay in the safety of Bangkok. They left the refugees unwatched and unprotected. When no one was watching, the wild wolves among the Thai soldiers, who were supposed to protect the refugees, came into the camps and raped and killed women and children. Sometimes the Khmer Rouge would also come into the camp to rob and kill people before returning to their hiding places in the jungle. We did not feel safe.

Ra, the woman who later became my wife, was a teenager while she was in a refugee camp. She became a victim of the Thai soldiers' games. One afternoon a small group of Thai soldiers entered the camp. They grabbed Ra for no apparent reason and kicked her all over her body with their army boots, as if she were punching bag. She fell to the ground and fainted. Her parents looked on helplessly. They forced her mouth open and shoved sand into it. She was bleeding and battered, crushed like a rose beneath the soles of dirty feet. They left her to die. They were brutal. They could have raped her, and no one could have done any thing about it. I thank God that they didn't.

CHAPTER 32

Miracles in the Camp

Life in the refugee camp was like being trapped. There was no other place where we could go. We could not go back to Cambodia, because we feared persecution and starvation. We could not go to a different country, because we had no sponsors. We needed a miracle.

Shortly after Meng and I were moved to our fourth orphanage center, a wonderful thing happened. One day Mom, who was living in another camp, went next door to Aunt Chek Chor's tent to visit her. A man was there, telling a story. He said, "In Camp Seven I saw a little boy about four years old, wearing yellow shorts and no shirt, all dirty, running around one of the tents. He looked lost, so I asked the occupant of the tent about him. The old man said that the boy belonged to a neighbor back in Cambodia. He had become separated from his mother and did not know where she was. He had found the little boy a few months before, living with a Khmer Rouge family. He knew the boy, so he paid some money to ransom him and brought the boy to live with him, hoping that his mother would come to find him. He was planning to keep him for a while. He decided that if the boy's mother did not come to get him, he would take the boy back to Cambodia."

This was exciting news. The description fit Thong perfectly. But Mom could not go back to Camp Seven to verify who the boy was. She couldn't get out of the camp without being shot by the

Thai patrols. She considered going to the camp by herself, but dismissed the idea as too risky. She considered hiring a man to go and bring the boy to her. But if the boy turned out not to be Thong, she would be in a very awkward situation. Camp Seven was not far away—perhaps twenty miles. But it seemed unreachable.

During the next few days, at her place of work, Mom mentioned the problem to the volunteer doctors from Germany. As United Nations workers, they had the privilege of traveling between camps. One doctor had compassion on my mother. He took his van and went to find the boy. He took a photograph of him and brought it back to show my mother. It was our brother! Mother confirmed it. The doctor went to Camp Seven again and saw Thong playing. He picked him up, put him in his van and brought him to Mom. It was a miracle! The old man who had found him was none other than Mr. Kre, our neighbor from Cambodia.

[As I wrote these words, I could not continue without pausing for a few moments to thank God for preserving my brother's life. I also went into the bedroom of my four- year-old daughter, Rebecca, and gave her a big hug and a kiss. She was asleep. She did not know what was happening, and she pushed me away. In those days, when Meng was lost, we did not know God. But He knew us. He must have sent several guardian angels to protect Thong during that time, to preserve his life.]

For almost two years my brother and I waited patiently in the orphanage center to see if someone from America would sponsor us. Each morning I hurried to the center to see if our names were posted on the bulletin board. I carefully read each name as other children jostled against me, pushing me out of the way so that they, too, could check for their names. Each day was a disappointment, but I did not give up hope. I kept myself occupied with school, studying Cambodian literature, mathematics and science. I read many books, because I wanted to learn.

At last, a ray of sunshine shone into my darkened world. I received a letter from Mother that said our whole family had been granted the privilege of being relocated to the United States! I was so excited. I felt like a prisoner set free, like a bird released from its cage. I clasped the letter tightly in my fist, got down on my knees and cried. I had never cried like this before. Tears of happiness were rare in my life. I savored the moment. Then I thought, *What if this is not true?* The news seemed too good to be true. *How could my mother get our family sponsored to America?* I wondered. I could hardly wait to meet her and asked her about it. To make sure that we really had been sponsored, I checked for our names on the bulletin board every day for the next few days. Finally I saw our names on the bulletin board. "Heng Ly Lim, Meng Ly Lim". Seeing our names on there was like nothing I had ever experienced.

God was so good to us. He allowed our whole family to be reunited. When my mother gave me up to the orphanage, I was sure I would never see my family again. Nor did I dream that we would have a chance to go to America. Our family and our hearts had been broken and trodden upon by evil people, but now it did not matter. We were together as a family again, waiting to be sent to the United States.

A truck took Meng and me to meet the rest of our family at a refugee camp called Mai Rut. We stayed together in this camp together for a few months, and then we were transferred to several more camps. The United States Immigration Service tests were strenuous and feared by all the refugees in the camp. Every candidate family had to go through their test. Any wrong answer could result in failure and cancel their opportunity to go to America. This was one test we didn't want to fail!

To prepare for the test, our mother gave us very specific instructions and information to remember. When I was growing up as a boy, she always told me, "Heng, if you tell people the truth you don't have to memorize lies." The information we needed to memorize was not lies, but it was not the truth, either. We had to know about our family's history and facts like birth dates and parents' occupations. My mother changed all of our names, and she did not remember any of our birth dates. She changed her maiden name and made up my father's occupation. She said that she did this to protect us in case another bad regime such as the Khmer Rouge came to power. We all had to memorize this new information that she made up. We took the test. We passed.

Before we were admitted to America, our family was sent to Galang camp, on one of the islands in Indonesia, for language and culture training. We stayed there for six months before leaving for America. A few months after arriving in Galang camp, I had a special encounter with my former enemy—the "Father" who had burned my hand. In the book of Ecclesiastes, the Bible says,

> To every thing there is a season,
> and a time to every purpose under the heaven:
> A time to be born, and a time to die;
> a time to plant, and a time to pluck up that which is
> planted;
> A time to kill, and a time to heal…"

I saw him walking out of the American Red Cross building. It seemed ironic to me that such a cold-hearted person would be working in such a place. I had about 10 friends walking with me to class on that day. As soon as he saw me and recognized who I was, he looked the other way and scurried off like a frightened kitten. The thought of revenge came quickly into my heart, but I dismissed it. Having revenge was not worth the risk of losing my opportunity to be with my family and to go to America.

I got my friends' attention. "Look! You see that man running over there?"

Their eyes followed my finger, and they answered, "Yes."

"Well, he used to be my 'Father' in the orphanage in Kao I Dang. He is a bad man. He caused me a lot of suffering," I told them my story.

"Let's beat him up!" one of the boys suggested.

"No!" I said. "To seek vengeance is of the devil; to be meek is of God." I quoted to them the Buddhist proverb I had learned as a young boy. *[The things I learned as a boy still surprise me. I had thought that some day I would pay that man back for what he did to me. But I never saw him again.]*

CHAPTER 33

Journey to America

The day to leave Galang for America arrived. We were to fly from Singapore to America. But to go from Galang to Singapore we had to ride across the ocean in a very old fishing boat.

The 40-foot, wooden fishing boat looked old and worn out. It should have been condemned and used as firewood. It was powered by an old diesel engine, which gave off a lot of toxic fumes. After about 40 passengers had climbed aboard, the water was only a few inches from the gunwale. The boat's roof was secured by rotten four-by-fours, which were connected by loose steel chains. I made the mistake of leaning against a side rail. When a wave shook the boat, I was thrown overboard. I grabbed a chain with both hands and held on with all my might. The boat dragged me along, and my dangling feet surfed over the water. A man saw me struggling and came over and pulled me back onto the deck.

Most of the passengers rode in the bottom of the boat—or, as the captain said, "the cabin." I stayed there, too, with my family, but the diesel fumes and the smell of vomit forced me to leave and walk around on the deck. I was careful to stay away from the rail. I had almost lost my chance to go to America!

None of the passengers wore a life jacket. I surveyed the horizon for an island, thinking it would be good to know where land was if the ship should sink. But they were all several miles away. At certain times no islands could be seen at all. Even though the boat was much bigger than any I had ridden on before, and I now knew how to swim, I still experienced fear. I had a flashback about the night my family was in the middle of Lake Five Hundred. I had cheated death nine years before. Maybe I could do it again.

Sometimes I tried to retreat into the hold, but always I was greeted by the foul smell and sick faces of people, who looked as if they were all drunk. The atmosphere drove me up onto the deck again to get fresh air. In the hold I felt as if I were suffocating, drowning in the odor of a dump.

Life is fragile and precious. Some people died from nothing more than a mosquito bite or from eating a leaf from a poisonous plant. Here I was, the survivor of a holocaust in which half of the population of my country had been killed. I wondered what it would be like to live in peace, freedom and opportunity. I tried to imagine what it would be like to live in America. I tried to concentrate, like a magician about to pull something unexpected out of his black bag. But with my limited knowledge, all I could see was a picture of the Statue of Liberty standing tall, with her torch raised high to show the way for wounded searchers for freedom, like myself. With my eyes closed, teeth clenched and my hand holding tightly to the boat's safety chain, I imagined the lady of the Statue of Liberty and her smile. Like many pilgrims who have come to America, I longed to see her.

The boat brought us to Singapore, where we stayed for a week before taking our final flight on a Continental Airlines Boeing 747 to America. It was the first time any of us had walked into a "flying object". We carried with us everything we owned. We had no baggage to check. Mom carried a couple of torn bags, which contained a few small, but priceless possessions that she had managed to keep. They included my father's wedding suit, an Omega watch and a few cassette tapes that had "Sin Si Samuth's" songs on them. (Sin Si Samuth was a famous Cambodian singer— as popular with our people as Elvis Presley or Tony Bennett with the Americans.) We had some pots and pans and a few sarongs and blouses and some books. Like migrating geese, who take nothing with them on their long journey, we were "migrating' to America.

As a child I used to gaze skyward from the rice fields and watch with wonder as airplanes flew high overhead. Now I was stepping inside one! Many different emotions bubbled out of my heart all at the same time—exhilaration, excitement, hope—and some fear. As I took my seat, I wept with tears of disbelief and joy. "We made it!" I whispered to my little brother, "We made it!" I bowed my head, covered my face with my hands and cried like a man who has just won a marathon. Ahead of me was freedom, opportunity and peace. At least that's what I had been promised.

The airplane brought us to the San Francisco airport. From there a bus took us to a refugee compound, where we stayed for three days. Then we flew to Oklahoma City, arriving at midnight on November 11, 1981. As we walked up the jetway, we didn't know what to do, where to go or who to ask. We walked into an unknown world. But— bless God!—in the crowd stood an Asian man, holding a brown board on which our last name, "Lim," was written in bold black letters.

"Mom! There's our name!" Cheang led our family to the man.

"Choom reap sur," the man said in greeting.

"Choom reap sur," we responded.

"Hello. My name is Saveng Si. I am supposed to pick you up tonight. I work for the United States Catholic Center, and I will take you to your apartment," he informed us.

"Cha!" Mom responded. (It meant yes.) "Thank you very much for your generosity, sir." Mom was grateful.

"Do you have any other bags or packages that we should pick up at baggage claim?" Mr. Si asked us.

"No. This is it."

"Follow me, please," he said. He took us to a little car that had the symbol of a Mustang on the grill. He opened the trunk and loaded our precious belongings into it. Even with all our worldly possessions in it, the small trunk was not full. Mr. Si opened the passenger door, moved the front seat forward, and told us boys to get into the back seat. All four of us were crammed together in the back seat; Mother sat up front.

Immediately I noticed a strong odor. I wanted to open the back window, but was afraid to do so. Mr. Si noticed and proudly said,

"This is a new car. It is a Ford Mustang. I just bought it last week. This is the smell of a new car." I tried very hard not to vomit in his new car. On the way from the airport to the apartment, I got motion sickness and became very dizzy. I held my hands together over my mouth and nose and concentrated on breathing, trying to control myself. As soon as Mr. Si stopped in front of the apartment, I leaned my head out the door and vomited beside his car.

Mr. Si said, "Sister, this is your apartment." He pointed to a big, red brick mansion in front of us. All of us were in awe. I thought, *This mansion is going to be my home? Surely not!* He opened the trunk, told us to pick up our belongings and led us into the building. The front door was unlocked. He led us through the carpeted hall and took us upstairs. He unlocked one of the doors and said, "This is your new home! Welcome to America!"

We were excited. We dropped everything on the floor and ran through the apartment to check things out. It was a one-bedroom apartment with no furniture in it. It had a refrigerator in the kitchen and a bathroom. I opened up all the drawers in the closet. There I found several small coins that had a man's picture on them. I thought they were valuable gold and placed them carefully into my pocket. Everything in the apartment was modern and new. It contained many things we never had seen—carpet, electric lights, a gas range, a refrigerator, a sink, a toilet, closets and a telephone.

The refrigerator stood in a corner of the kitchen. Curious, I opened its door and examined it for several minutes, wondering how this box could make ice. Did it mix special water with salt to make ice? As far as I could remember, I had never before drunk ice water.

While I was checking out the refrigerator, a gray-haired Caucasian man and an Asian teenage girl walked into our apartment without knocking. The man was in his fifties, taller than any man I had ever seen. He wore a black cloak, a white collar and black shoes. The girl wore yellow shorts that were, in my opinion, much too short. I was shocked by her appearance.

"Greetings!" the teenager said in our native language.

"Greetings!" we responded.

"My name is Suzan Lim. I am a Chinese-Cambodian. I am here with Father Joseph, the Catholic priest. I am his translator." Father Joseph had a gentle look on his face, and he seemed to choose his words carefully. I couldn't understand anything he said. When he finished his sentences, Suzan would translate for us. He said many things, but I didn't remember them, because I was looking at Suzan. I studied her from head to toe. *The American culture is surely different*, I thought.

Before they left that night, Father Joseph took some whole-grain cereal from a cabinet, and some white water in a gallon container. (We learned later that it was milk.) He told us that in the morning we could eat it for breakfast. That box of cereal lasted us for two years. We all tasted it the next morning and never touched it again. It was strange food!

That first night in Oklahoma our family was so excited that we stayed up until six o'clock the next morning. Then all five of us lay down and went to sleep on the living room floor. (We were probably also experiencing some jet lag.) As soon as we fell asleep, someone knocked on our door. We did not open it right away, because we didn't know anyone and were afraid. The knocking got louder. Through the viewer in the door I saw an old lady pacing back and forth in front of the door.

I opened the door for her. Without hesitation she pushed the door wide open, startling my mother and brothers. She pulled the blanket off of them and said something we didn't understand. We had a mad woman in our house, trying to tell us something in a language we did not understand! When she realized that we could not understand her, she took my older brother and me by the hand and led us out of the apartment. She took us down the long hallway, down the stairs and out to the parking lot behind the apartment building. She pointed to the trash on the lawn and around the big metal dumpster. She picked up trash and demanded that we do the same. She murmured to herself, "Lazy!!" while watching us picking up the wet trash.

"Who is this woman?" I asked Cheang. "Why is she so mean? Cheang understood more English than I, but he would not talk to her. The November morning was cold. The grass was brown and covered with frost, and the trees had no leaves. Except for the few evergreen trees around the building, the whole neighborhood was brown and dead. *What kind of land is this?* I began to wonder. *Everything is dead.*

The shrill voice of this strange lady brought me back to reality. "Pick up trash!" *What sort of people live here?* I wondered. The cold wind bit into my skin and made my fingers hurt. This was the coldest temperature I had ever experienced. As soon as Cheang and I had finished our chore, the lady left.

Mr. Si came that morning to take us shopping for food. He asked, "Did you see a lady here this morning?"

"Yes," we replied, with great curiosity.

"She is Sister Ann, the Catholic nun who is in charge of the United States Catholic Center. She is responsible for your family being here." He talked highly about her. He explained that the U.S.C.C. was an organization that sponsored thousands of refugees who wanted to come to America. We are forever grateful for their kindness. They bought the airplane tickets for us and gave us two hundred dollars each for food, utilities and rent. (After we got jobs, we paid them back.)

CHAPTER 34

Getting Started in America

I remember the first time Mr. Si took us to the store to buy food. I was in shock. I had never seen so much food under one roof! In that Safeway store I saw fruits, vegetables, meat, milk and many other things as beautifully displayed as paintings on the wall of a museum. The delicious aroma of red and golden apples caught my attention. When we were in Cambodia, my mother had said, "Apples are only for the rich." I had heard about them, but having never seen one, I could only imagine how they looked and tasted. Now I could see and smell and touch them—maybe even taste one. Our whole family went shopping together. For us it was like a tour in a museum of food.

"Thong! Look at all the chicken eggs!" I exclaimed.

"Wow!" he responded excitedly. The shopping cart amazed me. Instead of carrying things, I could place them in the cart. I was sure that whoever had invented it was a genius. We were quite a sight to people in the store. We had no shoes. We were still wearing our Cambodian clothes. My pants zipper was not zipped; it was broken and had to be held closed with safety pins. My Mother wore her sarong and a blouse. Our hair was in desperate need of trimming. But our behavior was calm and proper. We stayed together and spoke softly to each other as people stared at us. We bought a whole chicken, several pounds of cabbage, carrots, rice, salt and sugar. The chicken lasted a whole week.

Each day Mom boiled a piece of chicken with a lot of cabbage and a carrot.

Our family could not have survived in the new country without the help of many people. We could not speak the language. We didn't know the culture. We didn't have a car. We were like a blind man, groping about in a strange place. It was somewhat like being in the jungle. But God sent us some compassionate and kind-spirited clergymen and some families to rescue us.

Father Shaw and Father Gilmore, leaders of the All Souls Episcopal Church in Oklahoma City, along with the Harrington and Denman families helped us greatly to get settled in our new land. The congregation of that church opened their hearts to us, giving us clothes, furniture, shoes, socks, cooking utensils and school supplies. But much more valuable than the material things, the Harrington and Denman families gave us their time.

John and Carole Harrington had two children—Kathy, a cute, freckle-faced girl, and a four-year-old boy, Little John. Carole took us everywhere—to the Federal building to get Social Security checks, to the grocery store, to the laundromat and to school, so that we could enroll for classes. The Denmans and Harringtons took turns picking us up for Sunday morning church. We are so grateful for godly people like the Denmans and the Harringtons. Without them, getting settled in a new world would have been intolerably difficult.

I was sixteen years old when I came to America, but had only a second-grade Cambodian education. Most American teenagers would have finished 11 years of education already. I was so far behind! Realizing that all of her children needed more time for schooling, my Mother changed our birth dates so that we would seem younger than our real age. Cheang was placed in the tenth grade, and I in eighth. Meng went to the sixth grade, and Thong to first grade.

A few days after we arrived in Oklahoma, The Harringtons and Denmans came to help us. John Harrington was a successful attorney with the Little, Circle law firm. His wife, Carole, was a tall, beautiful, articulate stay-at-home mother. Carole enunciated each English word as clearly as crystal. One would think she was an English professor. She was always well dressed and kept her high-heeled shoes polished. Her face was always happy and meticulously adorned with just the right amount of makeup. She wore shoulder-length hair. Further, she seemed to have a perfect family, a dream family such as I wished to have in the future. But Carole's beauty was much more than skin deep. Of all the people who helped us, she spent the most time with our family, making sure we could adjust to a new life in a new country.

"Say Guech, let me take you to the Laundromat to wash your clothes," Carole would say, speaking slowly and clearly to my mother.

"Lee Cheang! Ly Heng and Ly Meng and Ly Thong, come also!" She pronounced each of our names perfectly, with no foreign accent. We put our clothes into the trunk of her Chevy Impala and went to the Laundromat. *What is a Laundromat?* I wondered. *How can a machine wash clothes? Does it have hands, like a robot, to scrub and rinse?* I was full of questions about modern conveniences. Carole explained how to wash clothes. She buttoned the shirts, zipped the pants and separated the colors to prevent bleeding of the dyes.

When we returned to our apartment, Carole showed us that strange new device that would allow us to communicate over long distances. It was a rotary telephone. We had never seen one. We all stood around it with awe, wondering how a machine could transport a voice through a wire. "Your telephone number is 528-6831," she said. "Be sure to remember it. And your address is 505 Northwest 27th, Apartment 6. If you get lost, you tell that to a policeman or call home."

Cheang went for a walk to check out our new community. He was gone for several hours. Mom began to ask us where he was. He had gotten lost. He went into a Seven-Eleven store and called us from a pay phone. Our family got really excited when the telephone rang. We picked up the phone and heard Cheang saying that he was lost and needed Carole to come and pick him up at the Seven-Eleven. I knew that the store was only a block away, so I ran through the hallway of the apartment building and looked out the window. There stood Cheang in a phone booth!

Things were so different for us then. Anxiety about the new environment crippled our minds. Fear was a constant companion we slept with at night. I thank God for people like Carole. To help us become familiar with our new place, Carole took us in her car and showed us around the neighborhood. She took me to Harding Middle School, a school where I spent five months in 8th grade. She showed me the way to walk home, so that I would not get lost. Cheang rode a bus to high school. Meng and Thong went to Edgemere Elementary School only two blocks away from home.

Knowing very little of anything at that point of my life, I went back to school. People looked at me very strangely. Of course I was strange. I didn't wear the type of clothes and shoes they wore, and I had long hair. I looked like a jungle boy. Who wouldn't look at me strangely? There I saw Suzan with her friends. I was so shy that I could not say a word to anyone without being afraid. Every day I was the first one to get to school and the first one to hurry back home. In class I couldn't understand a word the teacher said. There was one class I really liked—English As A Second Language. In that class there was a teacher who could communicate to me in my language. That class was a shelter in which I took refuge in school.

One day after school Suzan Denman waited for me in her "woody" station wagon. I was surprised to see her. She said, "Ly Heng, come on. I got you a job." I could hardly understand what she said, but I figured out that she was taking me to apply for a job. My first job in America was to be a grocery bag boy at Heritage Market, making $3.00 per hour. Mr. Keith Higgin, the owner, said that I should come to work every day after school and all day Saturday. I was happy to get a job, and I did my very best to please my boss and the customers.

Mom started working at an El Chico restaurant as a dishwasher and cleaner. She cleaned and mopped the floor of the restaurant until really late at night. She was 37 years old then, but several times people mistook her for my sister. She was a very attractive woman, and yet very skinny—not well suited for such a rigorous job.

At nine-thirty or ten o'clock at night Mom walked home from work all alone. Sometimes she carried a stick in her hand to scare dogs away or to protect herself from strangers. She had to walk through an unsafe part of town. In the snow, ice, and cold—even when the temperature was below zero—my mother walked to work and back. Sometimes I walked with her. We both wrapped scarves around our faces to protect us from the freezing wind. We walked along Robinson Street, slipping and sliding, then took a short cut through a park.

"Mother, are you not afraid of dogs?" I asked her one night.

"Afraid of dogs?" she replied. "No." I knew she was afraid of dogs, but she said "no" for me, knowing that I was frightened by the sight of dogs. "Son, when you see a dog chasing after you, and you run, he will chase after you and bite you." Mother pretended to be strong. She added, "When you see a big dog coming toward you, sit down, be still and courageous and stare him in the eye, and he will run away." I thought, *I am not about to sit down and let a dog grab my throat!* I thought my mother was kidding.

But sure enough, that night a big black dog saw us walking, and he barked. We both got scared. The dog ran toward us. I started to run, but Mother said, "Son! Stop! He will chase you." Mother squatted down with the big stick in her hand and waited for him. The dog came to a sudden stop when he saw that big stick waiting for him. He turned around and ran the other way. Mother was right.

It was very late when we arrived home. My brothers and I would often give our mother a massage to help her weary body get ready for the next day of work. Cheang also worked very hard to support the family. After school he rode his bike to a restaurant and worked as a busboy and cleaner. He worked two jobs. He normally arrived home really late at night.

Our family struggled, but our new life was much better than what we had known in Cambodia. Several Cambodian families suggested that we accept welfare and forget about the struggle. But we were determined to make it on our own. Besides regular school and jobs, we also attended language school to learn English.

The Harringtons and the Denmans faithfully took our family to church on Sunday mornings. We attended All Souls Episcopal Church for a short while, and then moved to Trinity Baptist Church. At that time church held no spiritual significance for me. It was a place to get help with the language. Many Cambodian refugees attended church to learn English and to get help from the church. In the basement of Trinity Baptist Church people could find old clothes, shoes, books and other items that had been donated by the American Christians. We did much of our shopping there.

CHAPTER 35

School in America

The following school year I was promoted into the ninth grade. I was shocked. I took no test or assessment to prove that I deserved promotion, but I was sent to the high school anyway. On my previous report card I had received A+ for Art, A for English As A Second Language and a C for the remaining classes. The educational system in America was not what I expected at all. The teachers did not receive the respect and honor they deserved. Students were undisciplined; they talked back to the teachers without consequences. Some students came to class unprepared, having not finished their homework. Some did not bring their books, nor paper nor pencil. They chewed gum in the classroom. I believe that I received some good grades because of my good discipline; I sat in class quietly, I arrived on time, and I never disrupted the class. I felt badly for the teachers, because they received so little honor from their students.

Most of those students did not realize what they had. They didn't take school as seriously as they should have. I am thankful for the love and encouragement my teachers gave me. Several teachers encouraged me to continue, even though I was so far behind with my education. Mrs. Gould, who taught English and French, said one day after reading one of my papers, "Paulette! Please take Heng down to the library and show him how to write in cursive." I was sitting at a desk next to the windows. Everybody stopped what they were doing and looked at me. Their faces said, *You are in the tenth grade and can't write in cursive?*

Paulette took me down to the library and, as sweetly as she could, took a book from the shelf, smiled at me and said, "Heng, let me show you."

Many other teachers and students helped me make progress in education. I am greatly indebted to them. The first few years of school were very difficult for me. Several times I wanted to give up. But when I would come home at night and see my mother suffering from her hard work in the restaurant, I was motivated to try harder in school. Mom would say, "Education is your only way out."

Sometimes at night Mom had me recite a poem for her to remind me of the value of education. Sometimes she started the poem, and I finished it for her. It went something like this:

> I learned to write the ABC's
> When I was but a child.
> My teacher taught them all to me.
> It took me quite a while.

> I was determined to succeed;
> I studied day and night,
> And prayed for God to help me read
> And do my lessons right.

> Now that I've studied very long,
> I'm grateful for my teachers.
> They helped me not to turn out wrong.
> Education is a treasure.

I learned a great deal in high school. Knowledge came into my life like sunshine into a dark room. When I graduated from high school, I was ranked 15th out of a class of 365 students. But it was not education alone that gave me confidence; it was the power of Almighty God.

CHAPTER 36

My Spiritual Journey

In Buddhism we were taught to perform good deeds so that we could be blessed in our future life. I was taught, as a child, that if I did good deeds in this life, if I gave consideration to other people, served them, had mercy on them, gave them money and avoided killing or hurting them, in the next life I might be reincarnated into a better person. But if I did not do those things, I might digress and become a lesser person, or even an animal!

When the Khmer Rouge took over and started killing so many Cambodians, I knew that Buddhism was not real. And I was a student of the high priest! I was raised in the temple. I had learned how to pray in Sanskrit. But at that time I came to understand that Buddha was not the God I was looking for. We were taught that good deeds would be rewarded by blessings, and that bad deeds would be recompensed by punishment. I did not believe that my family or I myself had done any evil deeds. And yet suffering and death came to us—and to half the people in Cambodia. There had to be something wrong. Here was a country in which the majority of the people professed to be Buddha followers. According to Buddhist teaching, killing was wrong. But the Cambodians who participated in the killing were getting down deep into sin. This caused me to think that Buddhism might not be a religion of which I wanted to be a part.

Buddha was a man. He was not a god-man. He was only a man.

He had a wife and children. He was a great teacher who was concerned about people's suffering and sin. He was the son of a wealthy man in India. One day he went out of his palace and saw the old people and others who were suffering, and he had compassion on them. He felt very distraught, and he said, "What can I do to help these people?" So in the middle of the night he ran away from the palace and went to seek for knowledge to save and to help people. It was through this, according to Buddhist teaching, that he was enlightened. Through his searching for the truth he became a very good man. His teaching proliferated, because people believed that he had found the truth. He set up laws and commands for people to follow. These are contained in prayers and books. People developed a high regard for Buddha. But he never claimed to be God. He declared himself to be a teacher. Yet as I was growing up in Cambodia and was being raised in the Buddhist temple, there were Buddha statues everywhere, made out of concrete and gold and lead and other materials. In the temple I saw people worshiping these idols.

When I was fourteen years old, I prayed that the true God would reveal himself to me. I was walking through the jungle with a group of people. I got sick, and they left me behind. I curled up inside a hollow tree. While I was there I cried out and said, "If there is a true God, reveal yourself to me." He helped me and saved me. He helped me go the rest of the way through the jungle and arrive home safely. But I did not know which God it was.

There is good in Buddhism. It leads people to do good deeds. But it does not lead people to search for God. The fruit of Buddhism is self-control and gentleness. But Buddhists do those things because it is required; Buddhism is a "do-it-yourself" religion. They believe that at the end there will be a scale. Good deeds will be weighed against bad deeds. You don't know, until then, what your future will be. It is impossible to have confidence about your future. According to Buddhist teaching, you can only hope that your future will be good.

Buddhism does not foster a family atmosphere or a sense of fellowship. We met with each other maybe three or four times a year to eat together and conduct celebrations. That was all. It was not like the Christian church, which meets two or three times a week.

The Buddhism practiced in Cambodia was not just Buddhism. The majority of Cambodians were into other faiths also. Buddhism, of course, was the main faith. But all sorts of other religions were considered part of Buddhism. Many people worshiped spirits. Some worshiped their ancestors, and some evil spirits or demons.

Some Cambodians believed in "objects." For example, they believed that the tusk of a hog could protect them from evil spirits or from harm. (This practice is also mentioned in the Old Testament. Rachel stole her father's household gods.) In my family we had one of those fetishes. I don't know where it came from, but my mother had it. It was a broken canine tooth as big as a man's thumb—an inch thick and about three inches long. A lot of people believed that it would protect our family. For a short while I believed in that object—that it would protect us. But after I cried out for God from that little hole in the tree, I stopped believing in the object. I came to believe that there must be a living God some-where—one that could hear, rather than being an object made of gold or concrete.

My father-in-law once had a Kon-Krah—a protecting spirit. Obtaining one of these involves a frightful process. They kill a pregnant lady who is in her first or second trimester and take her unborn baby to the priest. They roast the baby over a fire, wrap its body in silk and have the priest put some sort of magical spell on it. The baby's spirit protects whoever holds it. If danger is coming their way, the spirit will speak—not in an audible voice, but to the conscience of a person. And the person will know whether danger is coming from in front or behind or from the side, and they will know what to do. My father-in-law had one of these until he became a Christian. It looked like a piece of roasted meat wrapped in silk scarves. He carried it with him across the sea to America. After he became a Christian, he buried it. Immediately afterward his whole family got sick. But through prayer and Bible reading they were healed. The object had power. Some people were so well protected that they could not be shot. A person could shoot at them, but could not kill them, because they were possessed by a protective spirit. My fellow Cambodians were really into magical spells.

There were a lot of occult practices mixed in with Buddhism.

I first heard about Jesus when I was in the refugee camp in Thailand. But I did not have any desire or intention to learn any more about him. In the refugee camp there was a church, and I went to it. My whole purpose was to study English. My comprehension of English was poor, and I could not understand the meaning of Christianity. Although Cambodia was once ruled by France, there was very little Roman Catholic influence in Cambodia. The king was very strong in Buddhism. He opposed efforts to spread Christianity in Cambodia. Most people loved the king, and they followed the religion he preferred.

I began to realize that I should consider becoming a Christian when I saw the love and care and compassion and mercy that the American missionaries showed toward us as refugees. We had nothing, and yet they cared for us. We asked them, "Why are you doing this for us?"

They said, "It is because we love you." That was not understandable, because growing up we never knew what love was. While our parents showed us in many practical ways that they cared about us, they never told us they loved us. We were not affectionate people. So when people said, "We are doing this because we love you, and because God loves you," it was a shocking experience

After we came to America, we continued to practice Buddhism for a while. In our house we had a small altar. We had cans of sand and incense sticks. According to the Buddhist calendar, on certain days, just as we had done back in Cambodia, we would light the incense sticks, place them into the sand and say prayers to God. We never prayed to Buddha. Buddha never asked us to pray to him. It was a prayer to an unknown God. The Cambodian people in Oklahoma City celebrated the Cambodian new year each April thirteenth. Several hundred got together. Buddhist monks and priests came. Food was brought in and offered to the dead. The monks would say prayers, and there would be Cambodian cultural dancing and other cultural activities. Through all of this I had no peace, no joy, no hope, no love.

In fact I experienced conflict. I had a lot of bitterness in my heart toward everybody—especially toward the Khmer Rouge, toward the Cambodian people who had killed other Cambodians, toward my classmates in the American school, who belittled me and made fun of me. Some of them called us "boat people." They put bubble gum into my hair and into the hair of some of my friends. They provoked us to get into fights with them. With my temper and bitterness I was always ready to fight. I never turned down a fight, and I got into many of them. I kept this a secret from my mom. When I got kicked out of high school for a couple weeks, I went home and said to her, "Mom, I have two weeks of vacation for being a good student!"

Mom didn't know any better. She would say, "Oh, I'm proud of you, son!"

Our American benefactors took us to church. Most of the Cambodians who came to live in Oklahoma City kept a firm grasp on Buddhism and Buddhist culture. There was tremendous peer pressure for me and my family and a few other families who attended the Christian churches.

Several Americans were instrumental in my becoming a Christian. One that I can particularly remember was my Sunday school teacher. His name was Norman Cantrell. He was not a very rich man. He was not much older than I was. But he lived a life that was devoted to taking care of us young people. I was in the youth department, and I could see his genuine love through his deeds. He taught us about the Bible and about the God of the Bible, and he challenged me to read through the book of Proverbs one chapter a day—to read though the whole book in a month and then start it again. He challenged me to read though the New Testament. I was very faithful to church, even though I was not yet converted. I was very careful not to jump into anything. I wanted to make sure that this new religion, which at first I had thought of as the "American religion" was really the truth. Norman Cantrell and his wife Vicky took me under their wing and taught me the Bible. It was really hard for me to make sense of the Bible at first. The lack of English knowledge made it difficult to read through the Bible, which was full of "thee's" and "thou's". (I started out reading the King James Version.) At the same time I was studying Cambodian and trying to read the Cambodian Bible. I was also studying French. Between the three languages I was somewhat confused. But I was able to make headway. Reading and writing and not watching much TV helped with my education.

I came to America in 1981. About four years later I "officially" became a Christian. I'm not exactly sure when I came to faith. I was in a church that did not focus on knowing the time of one's decision. I was saved during a church youth retreat, at a camp in Falls Creek, Oklahoma. I was a junior in high school then—it was in 1985. I had been in church for quite a few years. I do not remember who was preaching. I do remember that thousands of young people were there. I was the ping-pong champion in that camp. We had a lot of fun. One of the things that I desired to do was to sing in the choir. It seems funny now, because I couldn't speak much English, let alone sing! My youth director, Norman Cantrell said, "Heng, when we are up there singing, and you don't know the words, just say, 'watermelon, watermelon, watermelon'. People will see that and think you are singing." And so for four or five years I was a "watermelon Christian." At least I thought I was a Christian. I was attending church, studying the Bible and going out on visitation. But I was never asked for any kind of a commitment to be a Christian. I read the Bible, and verses like John 3:16 and Proverbs 3:5,6 meant a lot to me. I knew that I needed to be saved. And maybe I was saved, because several times I had prayed silently, in my heart, in my own home, *God, I need you, and I am one of those bad sinners that you came and died for.* I loved God and desired to read his word and to work for him. But at that camp in the summer of 1985 the need to make a deliberate commitment was preached. A lot of people went to the altar to accept Christ as Savior. The preacher asked, "Is there anyone here who has not publicly received Jesus as Lord and Savior? Come forward." I went. My youth pastor was very happy. He was there at the altar and helped me pray. After we got back from the camp, I was baptized in the church. I knew, even before this, that my spiritual life was growing and blossoming.

From then on I knew I was a Christian. But one morning in the month of February, 1995, I got up from sleeping and was getting ready to go to work. A thought came to my mind, clear as crystal. "Heng Lim, you know the date when you were born. You know the date when you graduated from high school, from college, from dental school. You know the date when you were married. You know the date when your daughter was born. But you don't know the date when you were saved." This message bothered me. I thought, *The day on which I accepted Jesus as my Lord and Savior—the Bible says that's the day I was born again. I was there, and I should remember—the time, the day, the occasion, what I was doing, what I was thinking. And I don't remember the date.* So, without hesitation I knelt down on the floor and prayed, "God, please come and save me." Then I called my pastor and told him that I wanted to be baptized again. And I was a deacon in that church! I called him up around six o'clock in the morning and told him, "You'll never guess what happened: I just got saved!"

He said, "Oh, really? Then you must get baptized."

I said, "Okay. I will get baptized next Sunday." I believed that it was important for me to seal that decision.

As I learned more about being a Christian, I saw a complete change in my life. It came when I started to go to church regularly, read the Bible, attend the Bible teaching and prayer meetings, as early as 1982. I had more love toward people. I had more patience. I was gentler. I did not "fly off the handle" as much. My temper was not completely under control, but it was getting better. The Bible says that this is a sign of godliness. I fought less often. As I trusted God to help me in school and saw him enable me to make academic progress, I gained confidence and believed that God could do good things for me and through me. I learned Philippians 4:13. "I can do all things through Christ, which strengtheneth me." This was a very good verse for me, because being in a new culture was difficult. But God helped me. I graduated with honors from high school. I owe that to God's grace.

Becoming a Christian was not easy. I have thought many times, *Buddha has so many followers. Could Buddhism be right? Besides, it is the religion into which I was born.* Several times I have wondered, *What if the chaos had not happened in my life? Would I still be Buddhist?* But I answer no. I have had doubts. But the word of God quotes Jesus as stating, "I am the way, the truth and the life." There is no other way. Jesus is the only way. I do not stomp disrespectfully on Buddhist teaching. But I can say that as a Christian I have peace, I have joy, I have hope, and I have love. With Buddha, I didn't. And that's a big difference.

Being a Christian brings me many benefits. Ephesians 2:10 sums up how being a Christian benefits a person: "For we are his workmanship, created in Christ Jesus for good works, which God prepared beforehand that we should walk in them." This word "workmanship" is the Greek word *poema*, which means "work of art", "masterpiece." Being a Christian gives me the opportunity to better myself professionally, to achieve, to be my very best, so that people can see my good work and say, "There is something special about this man." Another verse in the Bible says, "Let your light so shine before men that they may see your good works and glorify your Father which is in heaven." The Bible encourages me to walk uprightly and professionally.

Because I am a Christian, I want to be righteous, to do my very best as God's servant, to walk in truth, to be an encourager to other men. A masterpiece is meant to be on display, not hidden in a basement. And the Bible says that we are God's masterpiece. I like to think that this is God's plan for me. Knowing that I have a master, a Lord that I look up to, helps me realize that I'm not doing things just for myself, but rather for my Lord. And I do them in behalf of my church. I do them in behalf of my family. So I am responsible. If I fail, I will embarrass my Lord, my friends, my family.

Being a Christian helps me to be a better husband. The Bible says, "Husbands, love your wives as Christ loved the church." It teaches me to give my wife unselfish, unconditional, sacrificial love—to take care of her, love her, have compassion on her.

As a father, being a Christian leads me to teach my children to follow the righteous way, to have a disciplined life, to respect older people, and to love other people.

I know that Cambodians living in America feel a great pull to retain the old culture. A Cambodian proverb says, "The blood will call, and the skin will shout." Memories of the past will draw one back to the old ways. I once thought that Christianity was an American religion. But this is not true. Jesus came to this world so that all might have life, and have it more abundantly. So it is not just an American religion. In fact, it is not really a religion at all, so much as it is a personal relationship between a person and Christ. Those who insist on holding to Buddhism are missing out. They are missing a blessing. They are "missing the boat." They are missing joy—all the great benefits that we Christians have. This is especially true for those Cambodians who live in remote places where there are no other Cambodians with which to have friendship. They are living a lonely life. When you are a Christian, you have a family.

CHAPTER 37

Career Choices

During my senior year of high school, the school counselor called me into his office and asked, "So, Heng Lim, have you thought what career you may pursue after high school?"

"Medicine, sir," I answered him.

"Medicine?" He acted surprised. "That is a good career choice," he added, after recovering from the shock. It seemed that everyone was surprised when I told them I was going to be a medical doctor. Some people even made fun of me for having such a lofty dream. I knew the dream was more ambitious than that of the average man. But becoming a doctor had always been my desire. I refused to believe this Cambodian proverb: "Short people can't reach stars."

Within a year after my family came to Oklahoma, we had earned enough money to buy our dream car. It was a silver 1980 Oldsmobile Cutlass LS four-door sedan. Cheang found it at a dealership in downtown Oklahoma City and took Mom and me to look at it. We were not educated about automobiles at all. We did not know which brands were better than others. Our sponsor told us that Oldsmobiles were good and that quite a few Cambodian refugees drove them, so we thought it would be all right. Mom, Cheang and I walked into the dealer's office with a bagful of cash—$5400—to pay for the car. We began to pull wads of bills from the bag and to count them out for the dealer. His eyes popped wide open, and he raised his hand and said, "No cash. We take cashier's checks only. Go the bank and buy a cashier's check with it." We went to the bank and waited in line. When our turn arrived, Mom dumped the bagful of cash onto the teller's countertop and asked for a cashier's check. We had much yet to learn about the culture and the financial system in America.

Shortly after we brought the car home, Cheang expressed a desire to go to Lawton, Oklahoma, which was about a hundred miles from where we lived. Two other Cambodian teenagers went with us. Cheang drove the car. I didn't drive until I was 21 years old. But on the way there, I wondered if we could go to a new town without getting permission from the government. What if the police stopped us? A hundred miles seemed a long way to travel just for fun. I was reluctant to go, not knowing that in America we had the freedom to go anywhere we wished. That trip was a turning point in my life. Finally I could believe that America was the land of the free. Knowing that I was not under bondage to a government made me very happy.

Cheang graduated from high school three years after we came to America. During this time he worked as an account receiver at the Southwest Radio Church, a Biblical prophecy radio ministry led by Dr. David Webber. Cheang also worked as restaurant busboy. I continued to work at Heritage Market. By adding together Mom's income and Cheang's and mine, we saved enough, by the time Cheang graduated, for a down payment on a house. It was with much pride that we moved out of the apartment and took up residence in our own house. Now we felt like real Americans. And just before we moved to the new house, we changed churches; we went to Northwest Baptist Church.

Immediately after I graduated from high school, Mom and Cheang and I had a meeting. Cheang said, "Heng, what are you planning to do?"

"Older brother Cheang, I am planning to go to college at Oklahoma City University."

"Heng, I don't think you should. I think we should work full time and overtime and help Mom pay off the house," Cheang said.

"No, I don't think so," I told him. "Education is really important to me. I would rather go to school and work part time. I will not stay out of school for a year. If I get out of school, I don't think I will be able to catch up. I am determined to stay in school. As a matter of fact, I have already enrolled at OCU for this coming semester."

"Mom, tell Heng," Cheang pleaded, asking Mom to back him up.

"I don't know, son," Mom said thoughtfully. I knew what Mom wanted. She wanted us to get education. At the same time she wanted to pay off the house. But the house was not my priority. I wanted education more than anything.

That evening Cheang realized that I was not going to quit school. He said to Mom, "I am working hard, as the oldest brother, to pay off our debt, and everybody is going to school. When they finish school, they will not give me any money to support me. I am going to school, too." A few weeks after this discussion, Cheang came home from work and declared, "God has called me into the ministry. I am going to Boliver, Missouri, for college. Heng, do you want my job? I will talk with Dortha Harvey for you. My job is easy. I have my own room and a desk. Sometimes I read books when I don't have things to do. I think it will be perfect for you."

I was surprised by my brother's decision, but I knew it was the best decision he had ever made in his life.

"What college will you go to, brother?" I asked him.

He shrugged his shoulders and said, casually, "Southwest Baptist University. It is a Southern Baptist University. I am going to be a pastor."

"A pastor?" I asked.

"Yes, a pastor."

"I think you will be a great one," I said, trying to encourage him.

"Thanks, Heng," he said. Then he added, "You are the smart one—the smartest in the family, I think. I know you will make it in college. You can be a doctor."

"Thank you, older brother. I will try. But I have heard that college is hard, much harder than high school."

A week before school started, Cheang and I packed our belongings and left for college, leaving our mother and two little brothers at home. Cheang went to Bolivar, Missouri, in a 1972 Chrysler Fury II that had been given to him by a lady who was a friend of our family. The car looked old. The engine made a lot of smoke and choked like a patient sick with emphysema. The seats were torn, the floor had no carpet, and rusty places in the steel body revealed the car's age. We all prayed that Cheang would make it safely there. God was good to him; Cheang made it to college in that car. But when he got there, the car was "dead on arrival." Cheang did not attempt to do any CPR on it. He sold it for $75. He had left home with only enough money for gas for the trip.

I packed all my earthly possessions into the trunk of my old car, a burgundy 1980 AMC. It was a little better than Cheang's car, but it had no air-conditioner, and the brakes did not work properly. I drove to the campus of Oklahoma City University and went into the administration building to enroll.

As I opened the side door of this massive gothic building and went inside, I saw an open door that led into an office. To my surprise, Dr. Peter Denman was sitting there behind the desk! He waved me in and smiled. With his gray hair, Dr. Denman appeared very distinguished, sitting behind a massive desk, with two book-shelves against the wall behind him. On the other wall hung several framed credentials and diplomas, one of which prominently displayed the words, "Dr. Peter Denman." He was on the phone. I sat on the sofa and looked around at his office. Then I realized how insignificant my educational experience was. But here I was, sitting at the college campus where I hoped to spend four years of my life. Dr. Denman hung up the phone and said, "Heng, how are you? Are you ready to start?"

"I am ready to start, but I am not sure if I am ready to leave my mother all alone." I was torn between my desire for education and the concern I felt for my mother, who would now have to take care of my two younger brothers without any help from her older sons. Dr. Denman had been a history professor there for a long time. He knew just about every detail of campus policy.

He said, "If there is anything I can help you with, Heng, don't hesitate to come."

I told Dr. Denman that, as a freshman at OCU, I was required to stay in the dorm, and that my belongings were in the car, but that I really needed to stay at home. He said, "All you have to do is have your mother write on a paper that you will be staying at home. I will sign it, and the dean will give you permission."

With a grateful heart I left his office to pay my tuition, happy that I could stay at home and take care of my mother and still go to school. I believe God providentially put people into the right places at the right time to guide my footsteps. Dr. Denman was there when I needed him.

Financially and academically I was not prepared for college. At that time OCU had the most expensive tuition in the state of Oklahoma. Oklahoma University tuition was $35 per hour; OCU was more than $100. But Dr. Denman told me that OCU was the best university to prepare me for medical school. And after exhaustive research, I found out that it was true. OCU pre-med students had a higher rate of acceptance into medical and dental or graduate programs than any other school. I was determined not to place a price tag on education. "No gold or diamond could be compared to the precious value of education," my parents told me as I was growing up.

At one time I was deprived. Now I was not going to allow financial hardship to deter me from my goal. I believed that God had placed a desire in my heart for education. Most Cambodian friends said that college was not for them; it was too difficult and expensive. They wanted education, but were unwilling to pay for it. Some of them married young, during their high school years. Many dropped out of school and took minimum-wage jobs. I do not blame them for such a decision. It probably seemed best to them at that time. But it seemed sad to me, because America has so many educational opportunities. These people had struggled against a river of horror, as salmon struggle during migration. Many died, like the salmon, hoping that their children would have hope.

Sam, a good Cambodian friend, said, "Heng, I don't understand the language, and I don't have the financial means, nor do

I have enough intelligence left to struggle to finish high school, let alone to go to college." Sam's words summed up what the majority of Cambodian refugees felt at that time. And I understood their feeling. I didn't blame them. They deserved a rest. Their families had been torn apart, killed and raped. Their belongings had been taken away. They had been starved for four years, made to work 16 hours a day and had watched those around them die in great numbers. They had sneaked through dangerous jungles. They had to do what was comfortable for them. Most of them believed they could not afford the "luxury" of education

While I was attending college, I worked part time at Southwest Radio Church— first as an accounts receivable clerk, taking over the position Cheang had left for me. Soon I was promoted to a position in the recording studio as audio engineer, assistant or "gopher".

My first year of college was a disaster. My grades were not good. Most of them were C's and D's. The only class in which I got an A was French. I was shocked to find out that my high school training was inadequate and had not prepared me for college. Dr. Branch, my major counselor, called me in to his office and "dropped a bomb" on me.

"Heng Lim, what happened to your grades?" He sat behind his desk, holding my report card in his hand.

"I don't know, Dr. Branch," I answered him honestly.

He cut me no slack. He said, "With grades like this, you cannot expect to go to med school." His words exploded inside my mind like thunderbolts in a storm. My sunny day quickly turned dark. I was frightened by this news. I sat up straight, tried to think clearly and pretended to be unshaken, trying to show Dr. Branch that I had confidence. I had learned long before that there is great opportunity in every obstacle.

"Dr. Branch?" I asked.

"Yes?" He sensed the seriousness in the tone of my question. "I will improve my grades. Think I can do it." I spoke with determination.

Dr. Branch said, "I expect you to. You can't go to med school when your GPA is 2.0 or less."

"Yes, sir," I agreed, feeling embarrassed.

"That's all now," he said, as he stood and extended his right hand to shake mine. The rest of that day I tried to figure out what I could do to improve my grades. Over and over I asked myself what I might have done wrong. *Maybe I worked too much. Maybe my English skills were inadequate. Maybe I didn't spend enough time studying. Maybe I am no better than my refugee friends.*

On the way home that night, I broke down and cried as I had never cried before. When my father died, I didn't cry. I thought that the well of my emotions had run dry long ago, but it hadn't. I needed this cry. It was a cleansing cry; it refreshed me like rain refreshes a thirsty land. After the cry, I poured out my heart to God, asking him to help me through this difficult time. I went home, quietly slipped into my room, and looked into God's word for comfort. I came across Philippians 4:13 which says, "I can do all things through Christ, which strengtheneth me." I read it again and again and claimed it as my life verse. Then I wrote it down and taped it to the door, where I could see it every day.

Before this academic crisis, I had been saved and baptized and had gone to church, sung in the choir and led other people to the Lord, but I had never recognized that Christ's power could help me in all parts of my life—including education. I had tried my best and relied on my own strength, but through this crisis I realized that Christ was interested in every area of my life. I re-read Philippians 4:13 aloud and put the emphasis on Christ: "I can do all things through CHRIST, which strengtheneth me."

Proverbs 3:5-6 came to mind. I turned to that passage and read, "Trust in the Lord with all thine heart and lean not unto thine own understanding. In all thy ways acknowledge Him, and he shall direct thy paths." Where it says "thine," I changed it to "my" and claimed that verse as my own. I claimed God's promise.

Prayer and Bible reading brought much comfort to my heart, but still I longed to talk to a person whom I could trust. I was tempted to speak with my mother, but I didn't want to discourage her. The thought of talking with my older brother came to me several times, but I didn't want to disappoint him. He had always told me that I was the "smart one." Everyone expected me to be the top achiever, the best boy. I was "from good stock."

CHAPTER 38

Girls

By this time my mother was making preliminary marriage arrangements for me. She wanted me to marry the daughter of a friend of hers, who lived in France. That is the main reason why I had studied French. I wasn't sure what to think about this arrangement, but I did not totally disagree with it. After all, arranged marriages had been the Cambodian tradition for many generations. That was how my grandparents and parents got married, and they did well as husband and wife. The first marriage in the Bible was arranged by God, and so was that of Isaac and Rebekah. But I was concerned about it. And during that summer of 1987, I picked up all my burdens and concerns and gave them to God. The Bible says, "Come unto me all ye that labor and are heavy laden, and I will give you rest. Take my yoke upon you. . .my burden is light."

As the rising sun brings light to a darkened world, God brought new hope, joy and peace into my soul. My life changed. I ceased depending on myself and began to depend on God and to live under the Holy Spirit's guidance. I did the best I could and left the rest for the Lord to take care of.

Also during the summer of 1987 I attended the annual Cambodian Christian Conference at Bolivar, Missouri. There I met a Christian young lady, a wonderful, beautiful, foxy, angelic Cambodian girl named Ra. I had never dated; I was guarding my heart for the right girl. Ra was "bone of my bone and flesh of my flesh." It was love at first sight for me. That evening I saw her getting out of a truck in the parking lot of Southwest Baptist University. My heart shattered like glass on concrete when I saw a man getting out of the same truck with her. She was beautiful and graceful, like a swan gliding across a glassy pond. She was a rose. He was the thorn! Later that evening she graced the cafeteria with her presence. This time there were two little girls with her, perhaps seven years old, one on each side. Her long, black, silky, hair had flowed freely down her back earlier in the day. Now it was curled and perfectly arranged on her head, exposing her perfect profile. She wore a bright yellow dress. My first impression was that the girls were her children, because it was not unusual for Cambodian girls to marry young. But they were her sisters. Her parents were there also.

That evening I made up my mind to find out who she was. I went to the source. Of course I could not go to her. Cambodian tradition forbids young men to speak directly to girls about love. I went to the man who had come with her in the pickup truck. I learned his name and room number, and that evening I went to get the truth. I knocked on his door. When it opened, he was there, along with another man. They invited me in. I greeted them and immediately got to my business. "Who is the woman that came with you, Noun?" I asked, politely.

"Her name is Ra." He appeared startled by my question.

"Is she your – your girlfriend?" I asked, stuttering nervously.

"No," admitted hesitantly. "She is a friend—like a sister." His voice was tinged with both pride and disappointment.

"Thank you. Goodbye." I left as soon as I could and went back to my dorm room. I lay down on my bed and tried to figure out a way by which I could get to know this girl. Finally I thought of a way to get around tradition, so that I could talk to her. But at the same time I wanted to do the honorable thing. I would have to get to know her parents first.

God must have orchestrated my life for me, because Ra's parents were occupying the room next to mine, and we shared a common bathroom. Was that an accident? I don't think so. I believe it was providential guidance. Jeremiah 33:3 says, "Call unto me, and I will answer thee and show thee great and mighty things which thou knowest not." I did not go to the conference that year to find a wife. My mother was already arranging my marriage for me. But the Lord knew my heart and my needs better than both she and I. The Bible says that after God created everything, he said, "it was good. When he saw man, he said it was "very good." And God, the master designer of the universe, knew that Adam needed a wife, and he gave him Eve.

For the next three days I spent a lot of time with Ra's parents and sisters. I gave them no clue that I was interested in their daughter. They were godly Christian people, faithful members of the Nazarene First Church of Rochester, Minnesota. Ra did not know who I was until the last day of the conference.

I was twenty-one years old, with no lessons in romance. I didn't know what to do or say. Love was like a jungle in which I was lost without a compass. I decided that I would have to trust God in that area of my life also. So I prayed to my heavenly Father for guidance. He had already showed me that he was interested in every part of my life. My faith had grown.

The last day of the conference arrived. The day was bright and warm, and so was my heart. It was a great day for taking photographs. And that is what many of the conference people were doing—taking pictures for souvenirs. We gathered at the fountain in front of the student union building. Noun was taking pictures of Ra and two other ladies, who were seated on a wooden bench near the fountain. I stood back and waited for the right moment to make my move. I had not yet spoken a word to Ra.

"One, two, three, smile!" Noun said, while pressing his camera shutter button.

I moved in. "Hi, Noun? Taking pictures?" I knew what he was doing, but I asked the question anyway.

"Yes, Heng," he replied.

"May I take some?" I asked him.

"Ask the ladies," he said, confusing my thoughts.

"Hi, ladies. May I take your picture?" I was timid.

They giggled and looked surprised. They talked with each other for a moment, and then Ra said, "Yes."

"One, two, three, smile!" I took several pictures with a camera that didn't work. It had neither film nor battery. It was our family's camera, and it had not been used for more than a year. So I missed my opportunity to capture Ra on film, but I did take a picture of her with the camera of my heart. Once I realized that the camera was not working, I politely thanked the ladies, dismissed myself and ran at top speed to Wal-Mart to buy film and a battery. When I came back, Ra was still at the water fountain. I politely asked her again if I could take a picture of her by herself. She answered with a crystal clear, soprano, angelic voice, "Yes." With that answer, she sat on the bricks next to the water fountain, tilted her head to one side and looked at me with those beautiful, penetrating brown eyes. I waited a few seconds to savor her beauty, and then took photographs of her with both my heart and the camera. This picture still hangs in my office.

After taking the pictures I thanked her again and asked, "May I have your address? If it is okay with you, I will mail your picture back to you after it has been developed." She wrote her address on a piece of paper: Ra Chhunn, 2047 Cypress, Kansas City, Kansas. When the pictures were ready, I wrote to her. We began our courtship by mail and phone, and sometimes drove to see each other. God knew exactly what we needed. We needed only to ask Him. God had prepared both of us, and He brought us together at exactly the right time.

I found that Ra had a wonderful testimony. She was a woman of faith, honor, determination and discipline. She possessed both inward and outward beauty. She was a woman of rare quality, a precious gem. She came from a family of six children. She was second oldest, as I was. Her parents had required her to accept many household responsibilities, such as cooking, cleaning and taking care of younger siblings. In regard to romance they said, "Ra must not be disturbed. She must go to school." Her parents worked all the time. Because of Ra's rare beauty, young men were attracted to her. It was hard for her to deal with that while trying to conform to the Cambodian tradition that ladies should not talk with men. After high school her parents expected her to marry a young man of their choosing.

"They never told me I was smart," Ra told me one day. "To them I was only a maid."

One day a handsome Cambodian man fell in love with her. She had feelings for him, too, but he was not the one her parents had chosen. When her parents discovered the relationship, Ra was severely punished, both physically and emotionally. She ran away from home and went to her beloved English teacher, Mrs. Marlene Stocker, who took her in as her own daughter and nursed her back to health. To this day Ra calls Mr. and Mrs. Stocker, "Mom and Dad".

Right after graduating from high school, Ra packed all her belongings, took the two hundred dollars given to her by the young man whom her parents had chosen to be her husband, and without saying good-bye to friends or parents, took a bus to college in Kansas City. I met her the following summer. I believe that her story would inspire millions of people and greatly glorify God. Now you know why I love her so much!

Regardless of the culture from which we come, our lives are shaped by our past, our parents, and our heritage. Some young people accept the traditional way of life without questioning it. But for us there were two cultures—Cambodian and American. We had to choose a path that would allow us to advance in life, to have some degree of harmony with the old traditions, and be in line with what the Bible taught.

CHAPTER 39

Cultures in Conflict

One day I was in Anatomy class, dissecting a dog. The smell of formaldehyde was strong. I had a mask on. Suddenly the slap of a newspaper startled me. I looked up. The professor held out the newspaper and pointed to the headline. "Heng, look at this head-line." The front-page headline said, "Two Cambodians Caught Killing Dogs to Eat in California." Then the professor asked me, "Heng, are you still doing this in America?" Everyone stopped what he was doing and waited to hear my answer. Of course, in front of them lay a dog.

"No, sir," I answered, somewhat offended.

"Have you ever eaten it before? What does dog taste like?" His questions grated against my soul like fingernails on a chalkboard.

I wanted to say no, but that would not have been the truth. "Yes," I said. "One time. And it tasted like chicken." They wouldn't have understood if I had told them it tasted like cobra or rat or cat, because they had never eaten any of these. Cambodians ate dogs, cats, rats and snakes out of necessity. When people practice some-thing out of necessity long enough, it becomes habit, and then tradi-tion. Some traditions are good, such as the eating of lutefisk to celebrate the New Year. Lutefisk is a salted, preserved, malodorous fish. The fish is boiled, spiced and served hot. That is the tradition.

In Cambodia people don't have much opportunity. They do what they do and eat what they eat because of necessity. Here in America we have better food. We don't have to eat dogs, rats, cats or snakes. We have opportunity for education. American culture and tradition does not chain people to a life of poverty or keep us from pursuing the excellent things God desires for us. Some people say that if God wants us to have blessings in this life, we will have them, regardless of effort. I believe that God does want us to "have life, and to have it more abundantly". But not everyone will experience the blessings that God intends for us. In John 3:16, Jesus said, "For God so loved the world that He gave His only begotten Son, that whosoever believeth in Him should not perish but have everlasting life." But not everyone has everlasting life—only those who believe.

Right after the Communist regime was ousted from Cambodia and driven into the jungle, barns full of grain and sugar were left unprotected. People were starving. Those who knew better went to the barns and took as much grain as they could carry. Those who were afraid and said, "What if. . .?" had nothing to eat. A tremendous opportunity can be at your fingertips, but if you do not recognize and seize it, the opportunity will be gone.

This story from the Bible illustrates how important it is to seize opportunities. Luke 18:35-43 tells the story of a blind beggar named Bartimaeus and his encounter with Jesus:

"And it came to pass that as he was come nigh unto Jericho, a certain blind man sat by the wayside begging: And hearing the multitude pass by, he asked what it meant. And they told him that Jesus of Nazareth passed by. And he cried, saying, Jesus, thou Son of David, have mercy on me. And they which went before rebuked him, that he should hold his peace: but he cried so much more Thou Son of David, have mercy on me. And Jesus stood, and commanded him to be brought to him. When he came near, he asked him, saying, What wilt thou that I shall do unto thee? And he said, Lord, that I may receive my sight. And Jesus said unto him, Receive thy sight. Thy faith have saved thee."

In response to the faith of Bartimaeus, Jesus gave him his sight. We don't know how Bartimaeus lost his eyesight, but we do know that he refused to be silent when he saw opportunity arrive. Many people tried to keep him quiet, but he knew better. He cried out for help, and the master heard him. Like the blind man, I felt trapped inside my culture and traditions. I cried out for God to help me. And as soon as I thought I had a great opportunity, people around me tried to keep me quiet. That is what the professor in my biology lab was doing with his embarrassing questions.

As soon as I returned from the conference where I met Ra, I took the film to have it developed. The pictures turned out well. I wrote a letter to Ra and told her what was inside my heart. I didn't get a response back from her for several weeks. I am sure the letter shocked her. Included in the letter was a picture of me riding a horse. On the back of the picture I wrote, "Please accept this cowboy picture. It is I, riding a horse. Please don't think that we Oklahomans are all cowboys and Indians. We are just like you, except that we ride horses to work instead of driving cars. Just kidding! I trade this picture for a letter and your picture. Heng. P. S. You like my horse?"

Ra called me. After that we started to write each other. We fell in love with each other without our parents' knowledge or permission. My Mom was curious and seemed to know something of what was going on. When she found out that we were serious, she began to tell me about her plans. She wanted me to marry the girl from France, a distant relative of her father's people. One day when Mother was talking to the girl's grandmother, she suddenly handed me the phone and said, "Grandmother wants to talk to you."

"No, Mother. I don't want to speak to her," I whispered. But Mother put the phone in my hand before I could refuse.

"Hi, Grandmother!" I tried to be nice.

"Hello, Ly Heng!" She spoke sweetly. "How's school?"

"Fine, thank you," I politely answered her.

"I have a granddaughter who is beautiful and smart. She is of Chinese descent just like you. She is studying pharmacy. She will make a perfect wife for you. After you marry her, she can come and live in the U.S." In one breath she had decided what my life should be.

I was speechless and could only say, "Uh-huh."

She continued. "I will bring her to Florida so you can take a look at her."

I composed myself and said, "Thank you, Grandmother, but I must focus on my education right now." I didn't want to tell her that

I had already found the girl of my dreams. "It is okay for you to focus on your education, but first you have to be engaged." She was really pushing me.

"I am sure your granddaughter is beautiful, just like you." I tried to flatter her and honor her. (I had met this lady before, and she was beautiful. She was the sister-in-law of my mother's father.)

"How about my big brother?" I offered her an alternative. "Or how about my little brothers, Grandmother?" I tried to get out of her scheme.

"No, I want you!" she insisted. She had known me when I was a child and had even given me money with which to buy candy.

"No, Grandmother! I can't!" I told her emphatically, and said, "Good-bye." Then I asked her to speak to my mother.

Mother said that Grandmother became very upset. She said, "Go ahead and give your best meat to a total stranger to eat and deprive your own flesh and blood!" Mom said that Grandmother would never talk to me again. I decided that I was not responsible for her feelings, and if her feelings were hurt because of my decision, so be it.

I believe that there are three decisions which are the most personal and which people must decide for themselves: the choice of career, the choice of whom to marry and the choice of what to do with Jesus Christ. By the time I was a sophomore in college, I had already made those three decisions. I am thankful for God's grace and for the men and women God brought into my life to teach me, mold me and help me confirm those decisions.

I decided then that my relationship with my Lord and Savior would be above all other relationships. Then I waited to see if the Lord would call me into the ministry, as He had my big brother. I had gained a firm Christian foundation while in the church youth department. Norman and Vickie Cantrell, my youth directors, were godly, Christian people who spent a lot of time disciplining me. While I was in college, Dr. Bob Lee, a local dentist, was my Sunday school teacher. Another blessing was the privilege of working with other Christians at Southwest Radio Church. The Lord used the people I met in church, school and work to influence my life in a good way.

CHAPTER 40

To be a Dentist

At work I met a man who helped guide me into my career. He
was the "least important" man in the whole building. He was
not an employee. Many people thought he was a hobo; he certainly
looked the part. George Ellis (not his real name) was about 50 years
old. He always wore checkered pants and a striped long-sleeved
shirt with the sleeves folded up to his elbows. George always kept
his hair trimmed. It had scissor marks all over it. He cut his own
hair. He always carried a brown Bible beneath his left arm. George
was always there in the building. Over a period of several months I
never found him gone. His food was delivered to him. He looked so
alone. My employer, Dortha Harvey, said that George must be left
alone. I could talk to him on my own time. People avoided him.

The building in which the Southwest Radio Church was housed
had been a large, brick Baptist church. Some parts of it were creepy
and scary. But George stayed there night and day. He slept in one of
the many upstairs rooms. Once I went in there to look for something and saw his place. My heart broke. I thought that no one
should live in such conditions. In a little corner of a concrete-walled
room, lying on the floor, was a twin-sized mattress covered by a
dirty brown sheet and a pillow. An open suitcase lay on the broken
box springs. On the windowsill was a Parkay butter cup with a
spoon, knife and fork. Next to it was a can of freshly opened tuna.
He must have scurried away just before I entered the room. Some of

the employees mentioned his name in conversation. They called him "The hunchback of Notre Dame."

George was about five feet, ten inches tall and weighed perhaps one hundred eighty-five pounds. For some reason he took a special interest in me. I noticed him looking through the broken window in the corner of his room when I came to work and when I left. He did that for several weeks. In the winter he used cardboard to seal the broken window.

How could such a man have such an impact on my career decision? One day I stayed behind after clocking out from work. George was sitting at a table in the middle of the large gymnasium, with books and printing supplies all around him. I asked him if I could sit down with him, and he nodded his head and smiled.

"George, my name is Heng—Heng Lim. You know, "Hang me high from a tree limb." I cracked a joke with him.

He smiled and said, "I know who you are."

"George, may I ask you some questions?"

"Sure," he said.

"I have seen some letters with your name on them. They say, 'Dr. George Ellis.' Are you a doctor? Please, tell me about yourself."

He grinned a little and said, "I've been watching you since you came to work here. How do you like your job?"

"I like it. It is a good job."

"How is your older brother?" He seemed to be really concerned about him.

"He's okay. I don't talk with him much. We are busy," I explained. Then I asked him, "Tell me why you live in this place."

He looked down, took a deep, painful breath and then said, "I have a house on the south side of Oklahoma City. My wife and children live there. I used to have a clinic where I practiced podiatry. I am a foot doctor."

"Okay," I said, and he continued.

"For some reason, several years ago, my wife turned my kids against me and sued for divorce. She served me the papers, and I refused to sign them. We went to court a few times, but I didn't want to break up my family. I love them." Tears began to run down his face.

"What happened after that, George?"

"She kicked me out of the house, and I took refuge in a religious facility," he said.

"I am sorry, George." I was not sure whether to call him "George" or "Dr. Ellis."

"That's okay," he said, with hope. "I am going to have my family back one day." "What do you think was the reason for your unfortunate circumstance?" I asked.

He looked at me straight in the eyes and said, "I spent too much time at the clinic and neglected my family. My priorities were wrong."

I had never thought of that before—that a man could spend so much time working and providing for his family that his family might not want to have anything to do with him. I was young then and did not have wisdom. From George I learned that while there is nothing wrong with hard work, one needs to have a balance between work and family.

Some years ago at our church Sunday School Teacher Appreciation Banquet I won a door prize, a beautiful stuffed pillow with words stitched on it. It said, "A hundred years from now it will not matter what my bank account was, the type of house I lived in or the kind of car I drove. But the world may be different because I was important in the life of a child."

My conversation with Dr. George Ellis that evening made me think again about my career. I wondered if I should become something besides a doctor. Proverbs 4:26 says, "Ponder the path of thy feet, and let all thy ways be established." I prayed for divine guidance. But I continued going to the same school and studying the same major. Let me pause here for a moment and share something important with you. College is expensive. Not everybody can afford it—especially the private colleges. But in America people can go to college despite their financial means. The poorer you are, the better chance you have of getting a good loan. And you can work some to pay for college. You can't afford not to go to college. My wife and I borrowed several thousand dollars to pay for college. Now we have good jobs, and we can pay back the loan. A loan is nothing more than the toll you pay to travel on the great highway of education.

Don't let financial obstacles keep you from getting the education of your dreams. Ra and I did it. We started college with only a few hundred dollars.

When Ra left Minnesota, she enrolled in Mid-America Nazarene University in Olathe, Kansas to study elementary education. She wanted to help young people. For the first few semesters she received student loans. The school found her a home where she could clean house and take care of children in exchange for a place to stay. At one time Ra worked three jobs at the same time. She said, proudly, "I worked at McDonald's, waited tables at a Chinese restaurant and late at night worked on a factory assembly line, assembling pumps. The pumps weighed 70 to 75 pounds each." The pumps weighed almost as much as she did! I could not imagine her beautiful, tiny frame picking up 75 pounds of machinery.

In her sophomore year, while Ra was working at the Great Wall Chinese Restaurant, Lincoln Randolph, a handsome, well-to-do man in his early sixties took compassion on her. Ra routinely waited on Mr. Randolph at the restaurant. One day he gave her an unusual tip; he invited Ra to come and stay at his beautiful house. He said, "I have a nice home, three bedrooms and I am by myself. You are welcome to stay there as long as you like."

Ra said, "I will come only if my friend can stay, too." Not long after that, Ra's best friend from Minnesota and her younger brother Sean moved in with Mr. Randolph. He became a father to them; they became his children. I had the privilege of getting to know Mr. Randolph and found him to be a gentleman, a man of honor and wisdom. He was a widower. His three children—two girls and a boy—lived on the East Coast.

Mr. Randolph once told me, "Ra came into my life at a most crucial time. I was lonely. Having three children here helps me." Mr. Randolph always carefully chose his words when he spoke. I am thankful for Mr. Randolph's compassion.

My sophomore year went better than the previous year, but my GPA did not improve much. I dreaded meeting Dr. Branch again. He gave me the same ultimatum. "You can't go to med school with grades like this." I began to have serious doubts about myself.

I thought about Dr. Denman and went to seek his advice. He invited me in as soon as he saw me, and we talked. He asked me some questions to help me understand what was hurting my academic performance. "Do you have a girlfriend? Do you understand the professor?"

"Yes," I answered to both.

"Do you study?"

"Yes."

"Do you finish your homework?"

"Yes."

After our conversation, he suggested that I should take an Effective Reading class during the summer to help me read faster and understand better. He said that "having a better command of the language" might help me improve my grades. That summer I took an Effective Reading class at Oklahoma State University. It was easy, and I earned an A in it. When school began in the Fall, I spent more time in the library studying. I doubled my time of test preparation. My grades went from C to A+. But during this time I did something foolish, which I regret to this day. I neglected Ra. I told her over the phone that I wanted to break up with her. I said, "I have no time for you, and I am not going to get married until I finish med school, which is eight years from now."

Ra cried. A week later she showed up at my doorstep with her best friend, Veda. She said, "Fine! You can finish with your school and education, but I am not going to wait for you. You are being unreasonable. I will be an old maid!" She cried as she talked. "Dr. Susan, up in Minnesota, offered me a job in her psychology practice. She will pay for my school and a place for me to stay while I get my masters and Ph.D. Do you want me to go back up there?" I remained speechless. That made her more upset.

"I am going to Minnesota and marry any man my parents choose for me. Is that what you want?" She piled guilt on me. "My mother told me not to get involved with you. She said that a Chinese man would not love me, a Cambodian, as he would a Chinese." She knew how to get to me.

"I am not Chinese! I am Cambodian! Don't you understand?" I raised my voice. "There is no difference between Chinese,

Cambodian or American when it comes to love." I toned my voice down a little.

"Okay. Prove it, then!" She looked straight into my heart with her big, brown tear-filled eyes. I understood then what John said in I John 3:18: "My little children, let us not love in word, neither in tongue, but in deed and in truth." I realized my mistake and begged for her forgiveness, and Ra and I were together again. That evening I took her to the lake. We sat by the water, and I sang her a love song. The next day Ra and Veda went back to their home.

Our relationship was mended for a while, but I digressed to my previous behavior. Like a rose that withers after blooming for a while, our relationship deteriorated. Part of the reason was a lack of time. Besides school, work and church, I had started a new project that would demand an hour or two every day for the next two years. I began narrating the Bible in Khmer onto tape.

After I was saved, the Lord placed an excitement and burden in my heart about sharing the gospel with other people. I knocked on the door of every Cambodian I knew. I visited their homes several times. Evangelism Explosion class trained me to tell the gospel, but I had a burden to reach the people in Cambodia, who were still living behind the Iron Curtain of a Communist regime. These people were illiterate, uneducated and lost. I was also somewhat illiterate with the Cambodian language. I had studied the language for only two years in school. I felt inadequate for the task of reading the Khmer Bible. The Lord knew what He was doing when He allowed me to work at the Southwest Radio Church, and when he placed the desire in my heart to reach the Cambodian people. "If God is for us, who can be against us?" In the Old Testament he used a donkey to speak. So here I was, fully surrendered to the Lord to be used to reach the Cambodian people, even to become a missionary. But the Lord had a special way of making it happen.

One afternoon at work I was minding the phone while the audio engineers were in the studio, recording the prophetic message. The phone rang, and I answered, "Southwest Radio Church. This is Heng speaking. How many I help you?"

"Hello, Heng." The voice was that of an old man. "I am Mr. Smith, calling from Indiana. Do you have the Bible on tape in different languages?"

"Yes, sir, we have it in English and Spanish. Which one would you prefer?"

"None," he answered. "Where are you from, Heng?"

"Cambodia, sir," I replied.

"Do you have the Bible on tape in Khmer?" he asked. (Khmer is the language of Cambodia.) "No, sir, there is no Khmer Bible on tape that I know of," I told him.

Then he said, "Would you consider doing it— narrating it?"

"No, sir, the language is difficult, and I am not literate enough. And it takes time and money." I gave him a lot of excuses, as Moses did.

He said, "I am sending you some money today to get started. You pray about it." And he hung up the phone. I thought he was joking until Dortha Harvey, the office manager, called me into her office and said, "There is a check here for you to start a Bible narration project in Khmer language. You can use the studio equipment and reel-to-reel tape recorder to record. Or if you want to, you can take the recording equipment home and do it on your own time. We will keep the check. Okay, young man?" I could not say no to such an offer. I spent every available minute studying for college, and the Khmer Bible. By the time I was about to graduate from college, the narration project was nearly completed. Through the Bible study I had to do in preparation for narration the Lord worked in my life, and I became a more mature Christian. I began to learn that my relationships with loved ones were more important than education.

Again I questioned my goals and dreams. Was I being selfish, or was I living for my Lord? Often the story of Dr. George Ellis reappeared in my thoughts—the story of a very educated man living alone in desperate conditions, hoping that his family would invite him back home. I became unsure about my dream of being a physician. I poured my heart out to God again, asking him to guide me. I placed my trust in God and chose not to "lean on my own understanding." Dr. Bob Lee, my Sunday school teacher, was a dentist.

He asked me if I was interested in dentistry. I didn't know much about dentistry, but I didn't want to offend him by saying no. Dr. Bob Lee said, "The University of Oklahoma has a career day to which dentists and prospective students are invited for a day of scientific presentations and food." He told me the day, and I reluctantly agreed to go.

Before the career day arrived, I asked Mother if she would ask Dr. Hawley, a heart surgeon for whom she had been keeping house, for an appointment for me. She did so, and I went to see Dr. Hawley at his house. Mom said that Dr. Hawley had gone to school to be a dentist, but had changed his mind and become a heart surgeon. His house was situated in a rich and exclusive neighborhood. I had taken my mother to work there several times, but this time I felt nervous when I rang the doorbell and stood in front of that massive door. I felt inadequate to speak with a surgeon. I was so glad when I saw my mother open the door.

"Hi, Son," she said.

"Hi, Mom." I was uneasy. "Bill is waiting for you in his study room. Come on in." Mom guided me through a huge living room. Bookcases reached to the ceiling on both sides of the fireplace. She took me to a little room where Bill was sitting. Bill was about my height, five feet, six inches, but built more stoutly. His face was covered by a gray and brown mustache and beard. He had a receding hairline.

"Hello, Heng!" He stood and greeted me with a handshake as if he had known me all his life.

"Hello, Dr. Hawley. Nice to meet you." I extended my hand to shake the hand of a man who saved lives every day, a hand that touched people's hearts and performed surgical procedures. I was not sure whether to give him a firm handshake or a soft one. I looked him straight in the face and gave him a manly handshake. "Thank you for taking time to see me, Dr. Hawley."

"You are welcome, Heng. How is school?" He casually talked with me.

"School is great. A few semesters back I had a class with your son, Brett." I tried to find a common ground.

"Oh, yes?" He acted surprised.

"Dr. Hawley, what do you think the future of medicine will be?" I asked him.

"Well, ten years from now a lot of things will change in medicine. Insurance companies will take over the health care and dictate to the physicians what to do and how and when to treat the patients. France and Great Britain have social medicine. America is heading in that direction."

"What is the closest thing to medicine that will not be affected by social medicine?" I asked.

"Dentistry is a great profession—and will be for a long time. It is autonomous. That means dentists will be in charge of their own operation and not have outside interference," he said.

"Really?" I had not given much thought to dentistry before. I didn't think that there was anything great about being a dentist. My only experience with dentistry came when my mother had a toothache and went to a dentist to have the tooth pulled. *Everybody hates dentists. Why would anyone say that dentistry is a good profession?* I wondered.

"In your opinion, which medical school is the best one to go, Dr. Hawley?" I asked.

"OU Medical school, of course! It is local and has a good reputation," he said.

"Thank you so very much for your precious time and advice." I said this standing up and extended my hand for a shake.

"Any time, Heng. Good luck." He walked with me to the door. "Bye, Mom." I waved good-bye to my Mom as we passed the kitchen.

On the way home I mulled over what Dr. Hawley had said. *Dentistry? I don't know anything about it. Why would anyone want to have such a career, looking into, and working in, people's mouths all day? It smells bad, and people hate you.* I hated to go to the dentist. During the next few weeks I prayed and asked God to direct my decision. "I want to be a medical doctor, Lord," I prayed. "You know I've wanted so much to be a surgeon since I was seven years old. Please help me." I prayed a selfish prayer. I also decided what I wanted and then asked the Lord to help me to achieve it. I had a strong will. But the Lord worked in my heart by allowing me to speak with some of my classmates at the university. Hao Nguyen and Laura Ousley, the two girls in my class, were working on their prerequisites for dental school. They had already been accepted into dental school. At that time I was ready to take the MCAT, the Medical College Admission Test, to qualify for med school. But the one person whom the Lord used to tip the balance of my will from medical school to dental school was my girlfriend Ra.

During one of our conversations that year Ra said, "Bong," ("Bong" means "sweetheart" in Cambodian.) "In my psychology class we have studied and found out that physicians have a high divorce rate. Also most physicians are on call all the time. They don't have time for family."

"I have not heard about the divorce rate, but I have heard about the working hours," I replied.

Then Ra dropped the "Atomic bomb" on me. It came down powerfully, like the one dropped on Hiroshima. She said, "I am not sure that I want to marry a physician." There was silence on the phone for a long time.

"What?" was the only word I could say. "Do you mean you wouldn't marry me if I were to become a physician?" I needed to be sure I understood what she was thinking.

"I am not saying that." She tried to explain.

"What are you saying, then?" I pressed for an answer.

"You may reconsider your decision about your medical school if you love me," she said. Then she hung up the phone. That night I stayed up thinking about everything. I thought about being an optometrist, a chiropractor, an ear, nose and throat doctor, a physical therapist and a podiatrist. Then Dr. George Ellis's face appeared on the screen of my mind. Like a movie my mind replayed the scene of him standing alone in the cold, empty building of Southwest Radio Church. In the following days, every time I went to work, George was there. My decision to be a dentist became final when Dr. Lee and I toured the dental school and participated in a career day. I became convinced that dentistry was the closest thing to medicine, and that it would be a field in which I could serve God with my talent, have a respectable profession and still have time for my family.

In the summer of 1990 Ra and I graduated from college with our bachelor's degrees and decided to get married. Yes, *we* decided; our parents did not decide it for us. We did go through some traditional "hoops" to satisfy our parents and our culture. Traditionally, the groom has to pay for the expense of the wedding, pay a dowry to the girl's parents and buy gold, diamonds and precious gifts for the bride. I had no money for that. We became engaged on the 4th of July in 1990 and got married three days later. That August I entered dental school.

CHAPTER 41

Goals

Peole need to realize that once we become Christians, God wants to take us up to the next level. God does not want us to just get by. God wants to help us grow, to enable us to bear fruit. Many Christians—both Cambodian and American—say, "Yes, we are saved, yes we have our name written down in the Book of Life, yes we are now on our way to heaven." But between now and then they are struggling with life. They are struggling financially, they are struggling relationally, they are going through divorces, they are having all kinds of problems—especially the young people. They do not have goals; they do not know what they want to do in life. I have a great desire to share with people that America is full of great opportunities. Because we have so many opportunities, people have great difficulty choosing what is it they want to be. We also have the freedom to become Christians. But many people who have made that decision still live a life of just getting by and struggling day after day. I would like to share something with people that will help them go farther.

To progress in any pursuit, whether religious or secular or academic, a person must have a goal in life. Michael Jordan is really good at basketball. He can make most of his shots. But if no one puts a goal in front of him, he will not make baskets. Some people like to go bowling. But if no one puts bowling pins in front of them, they will not score. They have only the burden of carrying a heavy bowling ball. Each Christian needs to have a goal. Having a goal has helped me a lot. When I was growing up in Cambodia, I was desperate. I didn't have anything. I just wanted to survive. But I had a goal, and my goal was to become a doctor. And when I came to America I thought, *With God's help, and with the great opportunity this country offers, I can do this!* And I took advantage of the opportunities. I challenge everybody to do the same thing—to set up a goal. Of course it must be a worthy goal. Perhaps you are asking, "How can I choose a goal? How do I know which goal is good for me? I would like to show you by using the four letters of the word "GOAL".

The first letter is "G", and it stands for "God". Does my goal include God? What does God want me to do? With what kind of profession will I be able to serve God? Is God pleased with me to become, say, a missionary? Is God pleased with me to become a medical doctor? The Bible says, "If God is for us, who can be against us?" So you've got to choose a goal that will glorify God. Some worthwhile goals are to be a pastor, a missionary, a doctor, a lawyer or a teacher. It could be anything, if God is in it.

The second letter is "O", and it stands for "Others." *Will my goal help other people? Will it benefit others?* If I choose something that I enjoy, but it does no good for other people, then my goal is useless. The Bible says, "Love your neighbor as yourself." I think it was Zig Ziglar who said that if you help other people enough, you help yourself, too. So everything we do should glorify God and help other people.

The third letter is "A", and it stands for "Ability." I must ask myself, *Do I have the ability to do this?* And if I don't have the ability, how will I achieve it? There are all kinds of opportunities here in America. We have student loans to help people go to college. There are scholarships. We can enhance our abilities. Some people have special talents, like playing guitar or singing. But we need to understand our limits. I cannot sing very well. So it would not be good for me to choose a singing career as my job!

The fourth letter is "L", and it stands for "Love." I should ask myself, *"Will I love to do that? Will I love it?* Dentists are known to have a high suicide rate. And I am a dentist. Being a dentist is a good profession. It is held in high regard. But it is also a high-stress job. Dentists spend eight hours a day looking into a little tunnel about two or three inches wide. People come to see me and say, "Doctor, I don't like you. I hate you. I don't like being here. You hurt me. I'm only here because I'm in pain, and then I have to pay you." If a person doesn't love what he does, doesn't serve God and doesn't feel as though he is making a significant contribution to other people, he says, "Well, I have the ability, but I hate this!" Then he says, "I make good money. I have a nice house. What is left for me?" Some dentists commit suicide, because they don't love what they do. They don't feel loved. They don't feel appreciated. Young people need to look at these things when they choose goals. .

Earlier I mentioned masterpieces. We are to be on display—to be admired as Christians. I feel that it's our responsibility as Christians to do our very best, to make our Lord, our Master look good. If we don't do our best, to make him look good, who will? In Ephesians 2:8,9 it says that we are saved by grace—that our salvation is not of works. But that doesn't mean that we should not work or do well. Ephesians 2:10 says, "We are his workmanship"—it talks about work. Someone said that faith and work go hand in hand. It's like traveling in a canoe or a boat. One oar is faith. One oar is work. It they are not both working, the boat goes nowhere. If faith doesn't show in our work, that means we are spiritually dead. And so as Christians it's our responsibility to do well. In order for us to be displayed for people to look at, we've got to look good for people. If we don't, people will look down on us.

I have several goals. I am enrolling in a seminary this next semester to study for a degree in ministry. One of my goals is to help the Cambodian people in America realize the opportunities that we have in this country and the opportunity that we have as Christians. Many people in this country are starving spiritually, emotionally and academically. There's a lot of cultural conflict between the adults and the young within the Cambodian communities. My long-term goal is to help with that. My wife and I have prayed about it. We have asked that God would use us and lead us. Another goal is to write books such as this one. Another goal is to travel, doing short-term missions in different countries. We also want to encourage pastors in different churches across the United States, as God leads us and gives us the opportunity. But our ministry will not be just to Cambodians. It will be wherever the Lord leads us.

CPSIA information can be obtained at www.ICGtesting.com
Printed in the USA
LVOW11s1855120614

389806LV00004B/887/P